Justice, Legitimacy and Diversity

Most contemporary political philosophers take justice—rather than legitimacy—to be the fundamental virtue of political institutions vis-à-vis the challenges of ethical diversity. Justice-driven theorists are primarily concerned with finding mutually acceptable terms to arbitrate the claims of conflicting individuals and groups. Legitimacy-driven theorists, instead, focus on the conditions under which those exercising political authority on an ethically heterogeneous polity are entitled to do so. But what difference would it make to the management of ethical diversity in liberal democratic societies if legitimacy were prior to or independent from justice?

This question identifies a widely underexplored issue whose theoretical salience shows how the understanding of what constitutes the primary question of political philosophy has a deep impact on how practical political questions are interpreted and addressed. What difference would it make, for example, whether the difficulties concerning the safeguard of human rights were couched in terms of the justice or of the legitimacy of the documents and treaties sanctioning their implementation? How should the issue of the quality of democracies be addressed whether one assigned priority to the justice or legitimacy of democratic institutions? Addressing these and other topical questions, the book offers a new theoretical angle from which to consider a number of pressing social and political issues.

This book was previously published as a special issue of the *Critical Review of Social and Political Philosophy.*

Emanuela Ceva is Assistant Professor of Political Philosophy at the University of Pavia. She has published on themes of procedural justice, pluralism and respect for dissenting minorities and she is completing a monograph on value conflicts in politics.

Enzo Rossi is Senior Research Fellow in Social Philosophy at the University of Wales, Newport. His published work focuses mainly on the theoretical foundations of liberal democracy, with particular attention to problems of legitimacy and realism. He is completing a book on the liberal political tradition.

Justice, Legitimacy and Diversity

Political Authority Between Realism and Moralism

Edited by
Emanuela Ceva and Enzo Rossi

Routledge
Taylor & Francis Group
LONDON AND NEW YORK

First published 2013
by Routledge
2 Park Square, Milton Park, Abingdon, Oxon, OX14 4RN

Simultaneously published in the USA and Canada
by Routledge
605 Third Avenue, New York, NY 10017

Routledge is an imprint of the Taylor & Francis Group, an informa business

This book is a reproduction of *Critical Review of Social and Political Philosophy*, vol. 15, issue 2. The Publisher requests to those authors who may be citing this book to state, also, the bibliographical details of the special issue on which the book was based.

British Library Cataloguing in Publication Data
A catalogue record for this book is available from the British Library

ISBN13: 978-0-415-59729-6 (hbk)

Typeset in Times New Roman
by Taylor & Francis Books

Publisher's Note
The publisher would like to make readers aware that the chapters in this book may be referred to as articles as they are identical to the articles published in the special issue. The publisher accepts responsibility for any inconsistencies that may have arisen in the course of preparing this volume for print.

Contents

Notes on Contributors

Emanuela Ceva is Assistant Professor of Political Philosophy at the University of Pavia. She has published widely on themes of procedural justice, pluralism and respect for dissenting minorities. Her most recent publications include articles in *Politics Philosophy and Economics*, *Political Studies* and the *Journal of Applied Philosophy*. She co-edited the book *Diversity in Europe. Dilemmas of differential treatment in theory and practice* (Routledge 2010) and is completing a monograph on value conflicts in politics.

Gerald Gaus is James E. Rogers Professor of Philosophy at the University of Arizona, where he directs the program in Philosophy, Politics, Economics and Law. His most recent book is *The Order of Public Reason*, published in 2011 by Cambridge. Along with Fred D'Agostino, he is co-editor of the forthcoming *Routledge Companion to Social and Political Philosophy*.

John Horton is Professor of Political Philosophy at Keele University, UK. He is the author of *Political Obligation* (2nd edn, 2010) and has published extensively on toleration and a wide range of issues in contemporary political theory.

Sebastiano Maffettone is Full Professor of Political Philosophy at the Luiss University, Rome. He has published on themes of international political philosophy, liberalism, human rights, bioethics and business ethics. He is editor of the Italian journal *Filosofia e questioni pubbliche*.

Simon Căbulea May is Assistant Professor of Philosophy at Florida State University. His present research concerns conflicts of moral and religious conviction in liberal democratic politics. He has published articles on moral compromise, political legitimacy, and moral duties in *Philosophy and Public Affairs* and *Ethics*.

Glen Newey is Professor of Political Theory at the Université libre de Bruxelles. He is the author of *Virtue, Reason and Toleration* (Edinburgh 1999), *After Politics* (Palgrave 2001) and *Hobbes and 'Leviathan'* (Routledge 2008) and numerous articles on topics concerning modern liberalism, such as toleration, political morality, pluralism and political obligation. During 2008–10 he was Visiting Research Fellow at the Helsinki Collegium for Advanced Studies, where his research project focused on the relation between toleration and security.

Valeria Ottonelli teaches Political Philosophy and Public Ethics at the University of Genova. She has been working on immigration and global justice and on the normative theory of democracy. She recently published a book on the procedural justification of democracy (*I principi procedurali della democrazia*, Bologna, 2012).

Enzo Rossi is Senior Research Fellow in the Social Ethics Research Group at the University of Wales, Newport. Most of his published work concerns the accommodation of diversity in liberal democracies, with particular attention to issues of legitimacy and realism. He edited (with E. Bardone) a collection on multiculturalism (*Oltre le culture*, Pavia 2004) and is currently completing a book on the liberal political tradition.

Introduction: Justice, Legitimacy and Diversity

Emanuela Ceva[a] and Enzo Rossi[b]

[a]*Department of Political and Social Sciences, University of Pavia, Pavia, Italy*
[b]*Social Ethics Research Group, Faculty of Education & Social Sciences, University of Wales, Newport, UK*

That a polity should be, in a basic sense, legitimate and just is hardly a disputed stance among political theorists. More precisely, the task – commonly considered crucial to liberal political philosophy – of justifying the social order to all those who are subjected to it is standardly seen to embody both elements of justice and of legitimacy (Nagel 1991, Estlund 2007). However, there is little by way of consensus regarding the distinction between the two terms. Some draw a connection between them by explicitly presenting legitimacy as a criterion of minimal justice (Hampton 1998, Buchanan 2002), or in fact by considering justice as what specifies the standards of legitimacy, in the sense that the only authoritative orders a state may issue are just ones (Rawls 1971). Other theorists have disentangled justice and legitimacy altogether by construing both concepts as separate components of the answer to a wider question concerning the overall justification of the social order and of political authority, e.g. by arguing that a liberal–democratic political order calls for a specific kind of interaction between justice and legitimacy, where neither is a by-product of the other (Simmons 1999).

The possibility to operate a conceptual and/or empirical separation between the two ideas remains controversial, but has been object of little discussion. This issue aims to fill that gap. More specifically, it investigates the nature of the distinction between justice and legitimacy as well as the possible normative fallout of different ways of articulating the relationship between the two concepts. In fact, as some of the papers will demonstrate, the ways in which a polity should respond to ethical diversity are a particularly poignant example of how different understandings of the relationship between justice and legitimacy can make a difference to the normative standing of various concrete policies.

That becomes clear if one considers the question – prominent in this issue – of whether justice or legitimacy should be the first question of political philosophy. For justice-driven theorists, ethical diversity constitutes a political problem as it entails disagreements over the values that should inform the terms and conditions of social and political cooperation (Galston 2002, Larmore 1987, Rawls 1993, Scanlon 1998). From the perspective of justice, the main challenge raised by ethical diversity concerns, in other words, the formulation of principles according to which the costs and benefits of social cooperation should be distributed to different citizens putting forward different and possibly conflicting claims. Accordingly, the appropriate response to diversity would be primarily about finding fair or mutually acceptable terms to arbitrate such claims. On this approach, a possible way to conceptualize legitimacy would obtain as a consequence or a by-product of the establishment of a political and social framework characterized in terms of shared principles of justice.

Legitimacy-driven theorists, on the other hand, would not be directly concerned with the properties of the terms of social and political cooperation. Rather, they would concentrate on the impact of the fact of ethical diversity on the justification of political authority and on the terms and purpose of the exercise of coercive power (Copp 1999, Beetham 1991). Put differently, the main challenge raised by ethical diversity concerns, from the perspective of legitimacy, the conditions to make the state's right to issue binding commands and to enforce them through coercive power compatible with and acceptable to a variety of citizens pursuing different and possibly conflicting life plans. This concern is crucial to theories of democratic legitimacy, especially those of a procedural breed (Christiano 1996, Estlund 2007). On this approach, the appropriate response to diversity would be primarily about devising the most effective way of realizing the normative commitments that ground political authority. Legitimacy-driven theorists may thus start developing a conception of justice only once the conditions for the exercise of political authority have been set out.

But, of course, that dichotomy is just a schematic exemplification of the relevance of the justice–legitimacy relationship, and as such does not exhaust the logical space of the possible articulations of that relationship, which this issue aims to disentangle. For example, a further, important thematic area that can be illuminated by an analysis of the relationship between justice and legitimacy is the current methodological debate between 'moralists' and 'realists' (Galston 2010, Geuss 2008, Williams 2005). Crudely, realists take issue with mainstream Anglophone political philosophy's tendency to conceive of itself as a branch of applied ethics, insofar as it applies abstract pre-political moral ideals to the practice of politics. Realists contend that political norms cannot simply be derived from ethics, if only because the content of our morality is – at least in part – itself a product of the exercise of political power. Now the issue at the core of this issue provides a new angle from which to consider the debate between realists and moralists: the paramount concern for justice that dominates post-Rawlsian political philosophy could be seen as a consequence of its moralism, whereas realists would maintain that an empirically informed account of legitimacy should play a greater role in normative political theory.

Against this backdrop, the papers consider a number of specific questions that broadly address two main concerns: (1) the extent to which it is plausible to separate the legitimacy and justice of a polity, to capture different demands in the justification of the political and social order; and (2) the ways in which the challenge of ethical diversity affects the acceptability of the terms of social and political cooperation and the proper exercise of political authority, depending on whether normative theorizing is couched primarily in terms of justice or in terms of legitimacy.

Specifically, the collected contributions engage with such questions as:

- In what ways relations of moral and political authority can be reconciled with persons' status as free and equal?
- How does political legitimacy relate to whether or not we consented to it?
- What is the role of the actual attitudes and beliefs of citizens, and of the social and political context in which they have saliency, in a theory of political legitimacy?
- Might unjust institutions still exercise legitimate political authority, and illegitimate institutions issue just commands?
- Are the qualities of institutional procedures relevant only for assessing the legitimacy of a polity, or is proceduralism also a sound approach to assessing its justice?
- On what principles should a distinctively democratic theory of political legitimacy be based?
- How should it respond to the challenges of religious and ethical diversity, at both a national and an international level?

What follows gives a brief account of the ways in which each contribution tackles those issues. The volume starts with Gerald Gaus's discussion of the relation between justice, legitimacy and diversity within the 'traditional' framework of the consent theory of legitimacy ('Justification, choice, and promise: three devices of the consent tradition in a diverse society'). Gaus builds his discussion on the twin ideas at the heart of the social contract tradition: that persons are naturally free and equal, and that genuine political obligations must in some way be based on the consent of those obligated. The Lockean tradition has held that consent must be in the form of explicit choice; Kantian contractualism has insisted on consent as rational endorsement. In his contribution, Gaus seeks to bring the Kantian and Lockean contract traditions together. On his view, Kantian rational justification and actual choice are complementary devices through which our freedom and equality can be reconciled with moral and political authority. For Gaus, we should not think that there is simply one way by which relations of moral and political authority can be reconciled with our status as free and equal. Accordingly, he defends three distinct devices through which freedom and authority may be reconciled: justification to others, social choice and promise.

All three aspects at the heart of Gaus's proposal belong firmly to the furniture of the 'consent tradition'. It is with such a tradition, broadly construed, that John Horton's paper takes issue ('Political legitimacy, justice and consent'). Specifically, Horton raises some doubts about the liberal answers, canvassed by Gaus, to the question of what it is for a state, constitution or set of governmental institutions to have political legitimacy. Horton labels the two main liberal approaches to political legitimacy as 'Kantian' and 'libertarian', focusing in particular on the case for decoupling legitimacy from principles of justice and on the place of consent. By contrast, Horton seeks to argue that, without endorsing a voluntarist theory, according to which political legitimacy is simply created by an individual consent, an adequate understanding of political legitimacy should take much more account of the role of the attitudes and beliefs of citizens and the social and political context in which they have saliency than most philosophical theories tend to do. This also involves acknowledging the limits of theory in determining criteria of political legitimacy.

Such a 'realist turn' is discussed further in Enzo Rossi's contribution ('Justice, legitimacy and (normative) authority for political realists'). Rossi takes issue with one of the main challenges faced by realists in political philosophy, namely that of offering an account of authority that goes beyond the notion of de facto authority. But is it possible to have an account of authority that is genuinely normative and yet does not consist of a moralistic application of general, abstract ethical principles to the practice of politics? As Rossi points out, political moralists or idealists typically start by devising a conception of justice based on their pre-political moral commitments; authority would then be legitimate only if political power is exercised in accordance with justice. As an alternative to that dominant approach he puts forward the idea that upturning the relationship between justice and legitimacy affords a normative notion of authority that does not depend on a pre-political account of morality. He then argues that the appropriate purpose of justice is simply to specify the implementation of an independently grounded conception of legitimacy, which in turn rests on a context- and practice-sensitive understanding of the purpose of political power.

The commitment to testing the plausibility of the idealistic aspirations of a theory of justice is central also to Glen Newey's paper ('Just politics'). In particular, Newey asks whether political justice can be encapsulated by procedures. To this end, he examines Rawls's tripartite distinction between perfect, pure and imperfect procedural justice, concluding that none gives a satisfactory account of procedural justice. For Newey, imperfect procedural justice assumes that there could be an authoritative source of justice other than procedures, while perfect procedural justice takes a double-minded view of procedure-independent standards of justice. That leaves pure procedural justice as an apparently decisionistic mode of deciding which outcomes are just. Newey believes that this at least avoids the confusion between having authoritative procedures, and procedure-independent standards that are also purportedly authoritative. However, he argues that even a political procedure that defines the extension of a term such as 'justice' will lack authority over it once its reference is fixed. Since Rawls's categories of procedural justice are taken by Newey to be jointly exhaustive, the problem of determining justice via political procedures appears insoluble.

Such a conclusion is disputed in Emanuela Ceva's contribution ('Beyond legitimacy. Can proceduralism say anything relevant about justice?'). According to Ceva, proceduralism may be viewed as a promising approach to justice on condition that we divorce the idea that the interesting point of having just procedures is their capacity of leading to just outcomes (the version of proceduralism discussed by Newey) and we recognize procedures as an independent *locus* for justice in its own right. To make her case, Ceva builds on a discussion of the distinction between justice and legitimacy: whilst legitimacy is often thought to concern the processes through which coercive decisions are made in society, justice has been standardly viewed as a 'substantial' matter concerning the moral justification of the terms of social cooperation. Accordingly, theorization about procedures may seem appropriate for the former but not for the latter. To defend proceduralism as a relevant approach to justice, Ceva distinguishes three questions: (1) Who is entitled to exercise coercive power?; (2) On what terms should the participants to a scheme of cooperation interact?; and (3) How should the costs and benefits produced by cooperation be distributed? Whilst legitimacy is taken to concern (1), justice applies to (2) and (3). Although, as Newey shows, the appropriateness of proceduralism is debatable in relation to (3), Ceva argues that it is well equipped to address the justice-related question in (2). And it does so by focusing on the inherent moral acceptability of the way in which persons are treated by the procedures through which they interact.

The connection between procedural principles and legitimacy is furthered, within the framework of democratic theory, in Valeria Ottonelli's 'Equal respect, equal competence and democratic legitimacy'. Equal respect for persons is often appealed to as the grounding procedural principle of democratic rule. Ottonelli argues that if this principle needs to account for the specific content of democratic political rights, it must be understood as respect for people as competent political decision-makers. However, the claim that respect is due to people as a response to their actual equal competence leads to conflate democratic legitimacy and substantive justice, rests on implausible factual assumptions and makes it impossible to advocate the effective equalization of political capabilities. Therefore, Ottonelli suggests that the principle of equal respect should be decoupled from such a claim and be rephrased as simply prescribing that people be treated or publicly recognized as equally competent. Ottonelli defends this interpretation against what she calls the 'publicity objection', according to which this take on the principle implies insincerity and therefore cannot serve as a public justification for democratic authority.

The last two papers in the issue operate within such a respect-based democratic framework to study the implications of religious and ethical diversity on the legitimacy of national and supranational institutions. In his contribution ('Democratic legitimacy, legal expressivism, and religious establishment'), Simon Cabulea May argues that the constitutional establishment of a religion can be consistent with an expressivist interpretation of democratic political legitimacy, even in the familiar circumstances of religious diversity characteristic of a liberal society. Even if the state should be neutral in philosophical debates about religious doctrines, according to May, legitimate governments are, within broad limits, morally entitled to act in ways that they should not. His contention is that at least some instances of religious establishment can fall within the limits set by the democratic conception of legitimacy. This latter is taken to be grounded in two main principles: the principle of equal standing, stating that all citizens must be able to participate in political processes on equal terms; and the principle of equal respect, stating that governments may only exercise political power in ways that treat citizens as equals. In particular, May believes that whether official religious endorsements disparage or exclude religious minorities depends on a number of contextual considerations, including the philosophical content of the religion in question, the attitudes of the majority, and the underlying purpose of the official status of the religious doctrine.

The challenges posed by diversity to justice and legitimacy are explored at a global level in Sebastiano Maffettone's paper ('Global justification and local legitimation'). Maffettone distinguishes between the concepts of justification and legitimation with a view to offering a normative standard for the foundation of human rights compatible with cultural pluralism. According to this distinction, justification is presented as an idealized, substantive and top-down enterprise rooted in the moral and metaphysical substrate of a specific culture. On the other hand (but in line with the accounts of legitimacy discussed by Horton and Rossi), legitimation has for Maffettone a procedural and factual connotation and derives its strength from the success of some culturally independent but historically situated practice (bottom-up approach). As, on Maffettone's account, justifications are always culturally oriented, reasonable dissent on justifications for human rights is unavoidable in a culturally diverse scenario. This is why Maffettone thinks that we also need what he calls legitimation: a recognized practice or a public experience of historical relative success on which there is (more or less) general agreement. Building on this distinction, Maffettone argues that justification and legitimation should be made complementary for the sake of cross-cultural dialogue.

As will be clear from that brief overview, the issue of the relationship between justice and legitimacy is multifaceted, as some degree of controversial stipulation is inevitable when dealing with such contestable concepts. Therefore the papers collected here are as much an exploration of logical space as they are a defence of specific substantive positions. Nonetheless, and in conclusion, we hope that this plurality of approaches and their varied normative implications demonstrate the fruitfulness of investigating the issue at the core of this issue.

References

Beetham, D., 1991. *The legitimation of power.* London: MacMillan.

Buchanan, A., 2002. Political legitimacy and democracy. *Ethics*, 112, 689–719.

Christiano, T., 1996. *The rule of the many.* Boulder, CO: Westview.

Copp, D., 1999. The idea of a legitimate state. *Philosophy and Public Affairs*, 28 (1), 3–45.

Estlund, D., 2007. *Democratic authority.* Princeton, NJ: Princeton University Press.

Galston, W., 2002. *Liberal pluralism. The implications of value pluralism for political theory and practice.* Cambridge: Cambridge University Press.

Galston, W., 2010. Realism in political theory. *European Journal of Political Theory*, 9 (4), 385–411.

Geuss, R., 2008. *Philosophy and real politics.* Princeton, NJ: Princeton University Press.

Hampton, J., 1998. *Political philosophy.* Boulder, CO: Westview.

Larmore, C., 1987. *Patterns of moral complexity.* Cambridge: Cambridge University Press.
Nagel, T., 1991. *Equality and partiality.* Oxford: Oxford University Press.
Rawls, J., 1971. *A theory of justice.* Oxford: Oxford University Press.
Rawls, J., 1993. *Political liberalism.* New York, NY: Columbia University Press.
Scanlon, T., 1998. *What we owe to each other.* Harvard, MA: Belknap.
Simmons, J., 1999. Justification and legitimacy. *Ethics*, 109, 739–771.
Williams, B., 2005. Realism and moralism in political theory. *In*: B. Williams, ed. *In the beginning was the deed.* Princeton, NJ: Princeton University Press, 1–17.

Justification, choice and promise: three devices of the consent tradition in a diverse society

Gerald Gaus

Philosophy Department, University of Arizona, Tucson, AZ, USA

The twin ideas at the heart of the social contract tradition are that persons are naturally free and equal, and that genuine political obligations must in some way be based on the consent of those obligated. The Lockean tradition has held that consent must be in the form of explicit choice; Kantian contractualism has insisted on consent as rational endorsement. In this paper I seek to bring the Kantian and Lockean contract traditions together. Kantian rational justification and actual choice are complementary devices through which our freedom and equality can be reconciled with moral and political authority. We should not think that there is simply one way by which relations of moral and political authority can be reconciled with our status as free and equal. I defend three distinct devices through which freedom and authority may be reconciled: justification to others, social choice and promise. All three are aspects of the 'consent tradition' broadly construed.

Consent in the social contract tradition

The twin ideas at the heart of the social contract tradition are that persons are naturally free and equal, and that genuine political obligations must in some way be based on the consent of those obligated. In the *Second Treatise* John Locke rejects the claim of Filmer – and the entire conception of the Great Chain of Being on which the medieval order was founded – that some people have natural authority over others, and thus those over whom authority is exercised have a natural duty to obey. 'Men being [...] by Nature, all free and equal and independent, no one can be put out of this estate and subjected to the Political Power of another, without his own *Consent*' (Locke 1960, §95; emphasis in original). Almost right from the beginning the ideas that persons are free and equal, and that political authority must be based on the consent of the governed, went hand in hand.

Over the last 30years A. John Simmons has brought home a simple but fundamental truth: while consent can indeed reconcile our status as free and equal with submission to political authority, the undeniable fact is that few actually consent to political authority. If we understand the 'legitimacy' of the state as 'its exclusive right to impose new duties on subjects by initiating legally binding directives, to have those directives obeyed,' and thus generating corresponding obligations on its citizens, and if such legitimacy requires that people have actually consented to such a state, it turns out that there are no states that possess general legitimacy vis-à-vis their citizens (Simmons 2001, pp. 137, 156). This gives rise to a certain sort of 'philosophical anarchist' position according to which while it is conceptually possible that there be such a thing as a genuinely authoritative state that imposes obligations on its citizens, as a matter of fact no present state generally meets the necessary condition – general consent has not been obtained – and so in that respect all states are illegitimate (Simmons 2001, ch. 6). Such philosophical anarchists maintain that citizens should 'act morally' towards each other but not accept moral obligations to obey the state (Simmons 2001, p. 153).

Simmons (2001, p. 140) acknowledges that Kantian-inspired views do not lead to this result. The Kantian stresses that that since each person has good reason to endorse the existence of states, because they are 'necessary for the realization of freedom and rights and justice,' each has an obligation 'enter civil society and accept the duties society imposes.' Thus, for a Kantian such as Thomas Nagel, '[t]he task of discovering the conditions of legitimacy is traditionally conceived as that of finding a way to justify a political system to everyone required to live under it' (Nagel 1991, p. 33). There is a type of rational consent here, since the justification is owed to each person, appealing to her ends and values. Thus, on a typical contemporary Kantian view, justification requires the hypothetical consent of all idealized persons, who endorse principles and institutions that conform to their own reasons. Simmons, in reply, insists that Kantians conflate the justification of the state (are states necessary for justice?) with their legitimacy (are we obligated to obey the laws of our own state?). Even if each could be shown that there are good reasons to endorse the existence of states, and even the existence of their own state, it would not follow that they are bound to acknowledge that the state has a moral power over them to create new obligations. Simmons (2001, p. 147) concludes that

> [a]ppeals to hypothetical choice, acceptability, or reasonable nonrejectability have a very different moral basis and force than do appeals to actual choice. [...] Even appeals to what ought to be chosen in the light of the individual's own interests and values are quite different from appeals to that individual's actual choices.

Justification via the consent of idealized agents who respond only to their reasons to endorse or reject is very different from legitimacy based on real people's actual choices.

In this paper I seek to bring the Kantian and Lockean contract traditions together. Kantian rational justification and actual choice are complementary devices through which our freedom and equality can be reconciled with moral and political authority. We should not think that there is simply one way by which relations of moral and political authority can be reconciled with our status as free and equal. I defend three distinct devices through which freedom and authority may be reconciled: justification to others, social choice, and promise. All three are aspects of the 'consent tradition' broadly construed. As all-too-often occurs, philosophers have succumbed to endless disputes about *which one* must ground authority and its power to obligate when, we shall see, all three are important ways in which a free and equal person can live under the authority of others.

Moral authority among free and equal persons: the role of justification

The necessity of authority: the instrumental and constitutive interpretations

As Simmons notes, according to Kant the source of political obligation is our duty to enter civil society.

> Although experience teaches us that men live in violence and are prone to fight one another before the advent of external compulsive legislation, it is not experience that makes public lawful coercion necessary. The necessity of public lawful coercion does not rest on a fact, but on an a priori Idea of reason, for, even if men to be ever so good natured and righteous before a public lawful state of society is established, individual men, nations and states can never be certain they are secure against violence from one another because each will have the right to do what *seems just and good to him*, entirely independently of the opinion of others (Kant 1999, p. 116; emphasis added).

Kant goes onto insist that justice is absent in the state of nature because each relies on his own judgment, and thus 'when there is a controversy concerning rights (*jus controversum*), no competent judge can be found to render a decision having the force of law' (p. 116). Thus Kant argues that individuals are obligated to abandon the 'state of nature' and enter into a 'juridical state of affairs' (pp. 114–115).

The claim that there cannot be justice among free and equal persons without a state is open to two interpretations: the instrumental and the constitutive. Locke clearly presents an *instrumentalist* view of the injustice that arises in the state of nature when each acts on his own private judgment about justice. According to Locke (1960, §87), in the state of nature, self-interest, passion, and desire for revenge lead people to misapply the law of nature, and over-punish perceived violations against them (§§124–126). Consequently, to secure a condition in which justice obtains, 'all private judgment of every particular Member' must be 'excluded, [and] the Community' must live under an 'Umpire, by settled standing Rules, indifferent, and the same to all Parties.' A system of political authority, we might say, provides an impartial system of justice, and so overall a more just order. If this is how the authority of the state provides for the justice lacking in the state of nature, Simmons's sharp distinction between justifying the state and submitting to the authority of the state makes perfect sense. To justify the state is to show that it performs the task of providing an impartial umpire, and so an effective system of justice. Realizing that, one can think the state that does its job is a good thing and be glad when we have such a state. It would not follow, however, that one should submit to its authority in the sense of acknowledging an obligation to do as it instructs (just because it instructs it).

Kant points to a much deeper sense in which justice is absent from the state of nature (an 'a priori idea'), one which leads us back to the problem of authority among free and equal moral persons. Stephen Darwall has recently stressed the way in which interpersonal moral claims involve 'authority relations that an addresser takes to hold between him and his addressee' (Darwall 2006, p. 4). When I make a moral claim on you not to ϕ, I am not making a request that you refrain from ϕ, or calling attention to my opinion that ϕ is immoral: I am issuing an imperative that you must not ϕ. If I decide that your action falls under the purview of social morality, I see it as my business that you refrain from ϕ-ing (Baier 1965, pp. xviii–xix). I claim authority over you in the sense of claiming a *standing* to direct your action. And I suppose that you are under obligation to comply (Gilbert 2006, pp. 103ff., 147ff., 245ff.).

And here we confront the core problem: how can one have the standing to command the performances of others while treating them as free and equal moral persons? You are claiming that they are obligated to *obey you*. Recall that for Locke, fundamental to our natural freedom and equality is that 'the *Natural Liberty* of Man is to be free from any Superior Power on Earth, and not to be under the Will or Legislative Authority of Man, but to have only the Law of Nature for his Rule' (Locke 1960, §22). To be morally free is to have *only* the law of nature as one's rule. This implies, though, that one is not also ruled by the private judgment of others as to the demands of the law of nature. As a morally free person one employs one's reason to understand the requirements of the law of nature, and one submits to rule by that law, which is the rule of reason. Moral freedom is not freedom from morality, but freedom to directly employ your (private) reason to determine what morality requires. Such freedom appears straightforwardly at odds with the claims by others to authority over you, which is fundamental to the practice of interpersonal moral authority.

Unless there is an authority endorsed by public reason – the reason of all – a moral claim is simply the attempt of one person's private judgment to rule over others. For the constitutive view, unless there is an authority that expresses a public reason – a judgment that you and I both share – the practice of interpersonal morality is inconsistent with our fundamental status as free and equal. Notice that on the constitutive view, philosophical anarchism leads to either moral nihilism or moral authoritarianism. If you say that public authority is well and fine, but you see no reason why you should submit your judgment to public reason, you are no longer able to proceed with moral demands that treat others equally. You seem to have two options. First, you might forgo moral claims entirely. So far as interpersonal morality is concerned, this leads to a sort of nihilism: you neither make nor recognize interpersonal moral claims. To be sure, one can still have personal moral ideals, such as 'I will respect others,' but such purely first-personal ideals do not constitute interpersonal moral claims – claims that others must do as you demand. The second option is to insist that these purely first-personal ideals based on one's private reason do indeed have moral authority over one's fellows, thus leading to authoritarianism. Because the philosophical anarchist does not appreciate that all moral claims are exercises of authority over others, his effort to reject submission to authority while keeping morality is ultimately incoherent.

The public authority of justified moral norms

The social contract tradition makes a very quick move from the conflict of private judgment about morality to the need for an umpire with political authority to judge all disputes about right according to an authorized public reason, to which all submit (Gaus, 2011b). However, as T. H. Green pointed out in his review of the social contract tradition (Green 1986, §113), Hobbes, Locke and Rousseau overlooked the fact that between individual judgments about individual rights, and the determinations of public political authority, lies the social authority of practices, norms, and conventions. We might think of this as taking seriously Kant's idea that the solution to the conflict of private judgment is to enter into *civil society* – while we need to avoid a condition in which each does what 'seems just and good to him, entirely independently of the opinion of others,' this need not immediately drive us into *political society*. When a moral rule *R* is a social norm it is commonly recognized as a rule to be followed within the group and in fact there is general conformity to it (Gaus 2011a, §10). It is shared knowledge that it is the rule of our group: each knows that it is our rule, and knows that others know it to be.

Now when a moral rule that is accepted as a social norm is also endorsed by the private reason of each free and equal moral person – each moral person's deliberative rationality – moral authority is reconciled with our freedom and equality. Suppose rule *R* is endorsed by the members of a social group *G* in the sense that G^* – somewhat idealized members of *G* who deliberate solely on their relevant values, ends, and personal moral intuitions – all have sufficient reason to endorse *R* over all the alternatives. It is true that what is endorsed by G^* will not be the same as what is actually endorsed by, or would if asked be actually endorsed by, *G*. Different theories of public reason relate *G* and G^* different ways, but in all plausible versions a member of G^* deliberates on the reasons to endorse a moral norm that her counterpart in *G* has, but to which her actual counterpart does not always pay attention. This is, I think, a far less controversial idea than Lockeans such as Simmons would have us believe. We are a complex combination of selfish and moral creatures: the moral system, we might say, has developed on top of an earlier selfish set of motivations (Richerson and Boyd 2008, p. 114, Freidman 2008, ch. 1). Morality is required just because our will does not always align with our reasons to restrain our will and abide by social rules. As a rational moral agent, to know whether a rule is one to which my private reason accords moral authority, a test which consults my actual present will ('Do you now choose the rule?') is inherently flawed, for it supposes that our moral commitments and reasons will be dominant in our thinking (rather than, say, narrowly self-interested reasons that induce us to bargain and bluff).

If *R* is a social rule that is endorsed by the relevant reasons of all, when I demand that you conform to *R* I am not merely employing my private reason to instruct what you must do: I am appealing to a commonly recognized rule that our reason endorses as a rule to live by. In familiar Kantian terms, the rule expresses legislation in the commonwealth of ends, in which the law comes from all and applies to all. In addition, when *R* is a social rule, it is shared knowledge among us that *R* is the rule to which all submit. Because the authority of the rule is self-imposed, the claim to authority over others is reconciled with the status of all as free and equal.

Moral authority among free and equal persons: the role of choice

The challenge of diversity for reconciliation through justification

Justification as a device of reconciling moral authority with recognition of others as free and equal falls short of a fully adequate reconciliation. In a diverse social world, in which individuals have a plethora of values, ends, and moral ideals, it is most unlikely that any candidate social rule will be endorsed by all members of G^* as the uniquely best. On any plausible account of the deliberations of members of G^*, they will endorse very different rankings of candidate moral rules. The only way to induce unanimity is to greatly, indeed radically, idealize the members of G^* so that they essentially evaluate candidate moral rules in the same way, as does Rawls's (1999) argument from the original position. The veil of ignorance excludes 'knowledge of those contingencies which set men at odds ...' (p. 17). Rawls then attributes to the parties a concern with primary goods that provides a basis for their common deliberation. Insofar as we consider ourselves as agents devoted to some ends, they are what we need. When abstracted to the common status of agents devoted to their own (unknown) evaluative standards (values, comprehensive conceptions of the good and so on), because 'everyone is equally rational and similarly situated, each is convinced by the same arguments' (Rawls, 1999, p. 120). So although the original position begins by posing a problem of collective choice, the problem is reduced to a choice by one person, and so there is no disagreement (Rawls 1999, pp. 120–121). Although a degree of idealization that allows us to model a person's deliberation about her relevant values, ends, and moral ideals is appropriate, an extreme idealization that reduces the deliberations of members of a diverse society to that of a representative, single, abstract, person ignores our real problem: the justification of authority under conditions of wide disagreement.[1]

The eligible set

In a diverse society, then, self-legislation inevitably leads to disagreement. If we take this problem seriously, we must revise the typical Kantian-inspired original justification situation. Instead of constructing a deliberative justificatory model in which all members of G^* concur on the same rule, we should suppose that the outcome of any plausible deliberative model among members of G^* will yield a set of proposed moral rules.

Let us assume that a member of G^*, G_i^*, proposes the rule R_i, regulating some area of social life that, given her values, ends, and moral ideals, is optimal. If she were the moral dictator – if social morality conformed perfectly to her private reason (as many moral philosophers seem to suppose it should) – this would be the rule that all would endorse as authoritative. The problem is that under any remotely realistic level of idealization, other members of G^* are almost certain to disagree that this is the optimal rule given *their* values, ends, and moral ideals. Other members of G^* must consider how well R_i stacks up against other proposals. To simplify, let us suppose that each member of G^* is able to order all proposals based on her relevant values, ends, and moral ideals. Having constructed such an ordering she has evaluated the proposals from best to worse in relation to how well they advance or express her values, ends, and moral ideals.

Not all the proposals, however, will qualify as eligible moral rules. First, following Kurt Baier, R. M. Hare, Rawls and many others, we must suppose that there are some formal constraints on what can constitute a bona fide moral rule. An eligible rule must have a certain generality, the rule must be public at least in the sense that its content can be taught to new members of the group, it must be determinate enough to resolve conflicts within the group about what is the correct action, it must generally be accepted that its requirements override personal aims and inclinations, at a minimum the rule must not be viewed as hostile to the basic good or well-being of any member of the group, and a person must be able to endorse the rule whatever role such occupies under it (Gaus 2011a, §15.2). Secondly, it is important to recall that to accept a rule as authoritative entails that others can *demand* that you comply regardless of your personal aims and inclinations, appropriately rebuke and punish you for not complying, and that you appropriately feel guilty for failing to comply. These are real costs of moralization: one allows that one's actions become the business of the public, and that you are to conform your actions to public norms regardless of your own proximate aims, and are answerable to others for failing to do so. Now a member of G^* will not only deem ineligible any rule that fails to conform to the formal constraints on moral rules, but as she reviews the proposed rules in terms of her reasons to endorse them, she must take into account the costs of moralizing an activity. At some point she will almost certainly decide that, given the extent to which some R_i advances her overall values, ends and moral ideals, these benefits are exceeded by the costs of moralization. She will thus deem any such rule ineligible as a genuinely morally authoritative rule that she can endorse.

Each member of G^* will, then, divide her ranking of proposals into an eligible and an ineligible set. Let us call S the socially eligible set – the set of all proposed rules that are not in the ineligible set of any member of G^*. If S is null there is no eligible rule on this matter: that would be simply to say that no rule R_i(1) conforms to the formal principles of right and (2) each member of G^* has reasons to endorse that outweigh the costs of moralization. Of course any Kantian theory must worry that this will generally be the result of moral justification – that would entail the dismal result that there is no such thing as a publicly justifiable moral rule. Kantian theory has, in my view plausibly, argued against this dismal result (where all we are left with is the choice between moral authoritarianism and nihilism), but then has pushed onto a much more controversial claim: S is a singleton. Given evaluative diversity this is most unlikely. A plausible Kantian view under conditions of wide-ranging diversity will be left with a socially eligible set S that is neither null nor a singleton. No social order has been able to exist without moral rules covering, for example, basic rights of the person, harm to others, and property rights. Effective moral rules on these matters are a great good, and this would be recognized by an even moderately idealized G^*. But there is no reason to think that there is only one acceptable moral rule to regulate each of these matters.

Moral equilibrium

Can a group of free and equal people come to accept a common rule, even though plausible justificatory models are indeterminate? Suppose that members of G^* take the results of the justificatory argument, and provisionally assume that it is the limit of the morality dictated by impartial reason. Morality, we might say, is indeterminate, specifying only a set *S*. Insofar as justification has had an outcome, it is *S*: what is common to *S* defines the set of actions that are certainly morally prohibited, required, or permitted. Beyond that, each is free to act on the moral rule within *S* she chooses. Now each person has two concerns: (1) to induce the group to come to adopt his preferred rule; and (2) to come to act on a common moral rule with others. The first concern is obvious; a moral agent has good reason to induce others to adopt the rule that, given his private reason, he thinks best. In addition, though, moral persons are concerned with converging with others on a common moral rule. Until there is a shared common rule, known by all to be the rule of the group, there cannot a real moral life that respects all as free and equal. Should all come to accept the same eligible rule, then, finally, moral authority is reconciled with freedom and equality.

Two members of G^* can be modeled as playing an impure coordination game. Figure 1 gives the game in its simplest form, a simple 2×2 game (numbers indicate ordinal utility, highest being most preferred).[2]

Should Alf and Betty find themselves coordinating on R_A neither would have reason to change his or her action. For each, given his or her overall evaluative standards, each has the most reason to act on R_A. Should they instead find themselves at R_B, each will then have most reason (given his or her evaluative standards) to act on R_B. Note that in neither case is either induced by some external consideration to conform to a rule that is not, from his or her perspective, optimal: consulting simply his or her own evaluative standards, each has decisive reason to freely endorse whichever eligible moral rule on which they have coordinated. When coordinating on R_A Alf can demand that Betty conform and, consulting only her own values, ends, and moral ideals, she will have decisive reason to conform; and if they have coordinated on R_B Betty can demand that Alf conform, and he will have decisive reason to act on it, considering only what he thinks his

		Betty	
		R_A in *S*	R_B in *S*
Alf	R_A in *S*	2 (Alf), 1 (Betty)	0 (Alf), 0 (Betty)
	R_B in *S*	0 (Alf), 0 (Betty)	1 (Alf), 2 (Betty)

Figure 1.

important – his own 'utility function.' And this even though, from the initial deliberative perspective, neither had reason to act on the other's preferred moral rule.[3]

A one-shot two-person game can give us some insight, but it is clearly an inadequate way to model the selection of a moral rule from the eligible set. The relevant coordination problem is not a single-play game, but an iterated game. We have a number of encounters with others, and each can be understood as a play in a series of impure coordination games over many options. Now in an iterated game a person's utility (this is defined solely in terms of her relevant values, ends, and moral ideals) is a combination of her utility in this play, plus her expectations for utility in future games. Thus a person might sacrifice utility in one play to induce play in future moves that will yield her a more favored result. Now in large iterated games a bandwagon effect manifests itself. As I have argued elsewhere, such large person-iterated coordination games exhibit a strong increasing returns effect: the more people come to embrace a particular rule, the more reason others have to also embrace it.[4] Even if one ranks a rule near the bottom of *S*, under a wide range of conditions one will have strong reason to embrace it if most others are acting on it.

This dynamic is illustrated in Figure 2. Starting out with a population evenly split between advocates of R_A and of R_B, individual choices and random events can lead the population to all R_A or all R_B equilibria. Which equilibrium emerges will be path dependent: at time zero there is no reason

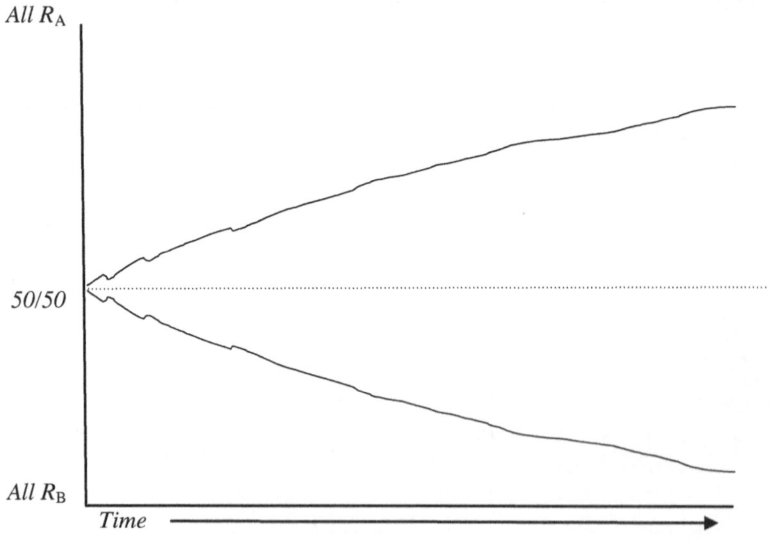

Figure 2.

why one or the other should emerge as the *unanimously chosen rule*. But once they have arrived at such a convergence, each member of G^*, consulting only her own values, ends, and moral ideals will freely act on the rule (which will be a Nash equilibrium). For our purposes what is crucial is that the contingent way in which large groups can come to coordinate on a common practice is no bar to there being a determinate morality that all can endorse given their evaluative criteria *once it has been arrived at.*

From justification to choice (and back again)

This very abstract model points to an important insight: a specific authoritative social morality that treats all as free and equal is to a large extent the result of the choices of its members. It is not *merely* chosen: not just any rule that a group might converge on is a genuinely moral rule. Bad norms, backed by punishment, can be in equilibrium: each may have sufficient reasons to conform simply in order to avoid punishment (Bicchieri 2006, p. 42). Punishment can stabilize just about any norm, good or bad (Boyd and Richerson 2005, ch. 9). Social equilibrium does not imply moral equilibrium, and the fact that a bad norm is in social equilibrium can make it very difficult to dislodge. However, when a rule in equilibrium is within the socially eligible set, it is both chosen by the members of a society and is acceptable from what Baier (1965) called 'the moral point of view.' The rule passes the tests of impartiality, generality, teachability, and so on, and is endorsed by the values, ends, and moral ideals of all. Each, consulting only his own values, ends, and moral ideals has reason to act on it.

A moral rule in equilibrium is not a collective 'we' choice; the group, *as a group*, does not choose its moral rules (cf. Gilbert 2006, pt II). Nevertheless, a moral rule in equilibrium is a social fact that arises from the interdependent choices of its members. As interdependent individuals, we choose our moral rules – at least, if we are lucky enough to actually possess genuine moral rules (§4). This is *a real choice of actual people*; not a hypothetical choice, or one dictated by impartial reason. To be sure, it is the choice of social creatures, who must take into account what others are doing, and cannot dictate to the group their preferred rule. Importantly, although the rule is chosen by members of society, taken individually in their interdependent interactions, and unless some rule was so chosen by the society there would be no effective morality, the authority of the morality does not depend on each and every person choosing the rule. Once society has chosen a rule, if the rule in equilibrium is also a member of the socially eligible set, we have created through our actual interdependent choices what impartial reason could not deliver: a uniquely justified rule. For once the moral rule is in social equilibrium (and is a recognized social norm), then all have conclusive moral reason to act on this rule rather than any other in *S*. Thus, having created a justified rule though our interdependent choices, we can then insist that all conform to this rule, for all free and equal persons now have conclusive reason to conform to this rule, rather than any other. That genuine moral authority is created by our choices does not entail than one who holds out, refusing to choose our rule, escapes the moral authority of our justified social–moral rule. In this fundamental sense, society consents to the moral rule to which we are all bound.[5]

Filmer long ago pointed out that, the 'plausible and dangerous' notion that all are free and equal appears to require that each and every person consents to authority, but it is impossible to imagine that all do so. And, Filmer insisted, it is not enough to say that the majority, even the overwhelming majority, have consented: 'unless it can be proved by some law of nature that the major, or some other part, have power to overrule the rest of the multitude, it must follow that the acts of multitudes not entire are not binding to all but only such as consent unto them' (Filmer 1991, p. 21). This has always been the Achilles' Heel of consent theory (Gilbert 2006, ch. 5). On the account advanced here, the consent of the majority – their actual choices in selecting a rule from *S* – has the power to bind the rest. Once society has consented to this rule, it becomes the sole rule that is uniquely rationally justified: it now is the one rule that all have reason to endorse. It is the only rule that all can endorse and which is able to provide the basis of shared moral life in which all are treated as free and equal. Each, consulting only her set of relevant values, ends, and moral ideals, has reason to act on that rule over any alternative. What was *ex ante* indeterminate, is *ex post* uniquely justified. In game theoretic terms, in the ex ante situation there are many possible Nash equilibria (in fact, every member of *S*); once a rule has been selected by society, it is in Nash equilibrium, and so all have reason to act on it.

Political authority, justification, and choice

The state as the protector, sustainer, and developer of social morality

Green (1986, §134) insisted that 'a state presupposes other forms of community, with the rights that arise out of them, and only exists as sustaining, securing, and completing them.' For Green, the great error of social contract theory was that it supposes that individuals somehow confront each other simply with their individual rights before the advent of the state, where in fact all states arise out of a pre-existing system of social morality and authority, and at least in the first instance their task is to protect, sustain, and develop this system of morality. Indeed, unless there is a definite pre-existing social morality, there is no reason to think that government can solve our problems. Until we can be confident that those with political authority will themselves abide by the norms of social morality, instituting political authority may simply leave us open to new forms of exploitation – those with authority may simple use the institutions to promote their narrow self-interest (Schwab and Ostrom 2008) or impose their personal moral ideals. Once we understand that interpersonal morality already supposes a system of social authority, the question is not whether free and equal individuals choose to be subjected to the authority of others, but whether, while endorsing social moral authority, they pull back and refuse to endorse political authority.

Although on many matters a society of free and equal individuals can coordinate on a common interpretation of a moral rule (and so, a rule specifying their rights), social coordination fails to fully secure a common authoritative social morality among free and equal persons for a number of reasons (Martin 1993, p. 166).

(1) Given social and technological changes, new cases may arise for which the social rule has no clear answer. Although we may expect that over a long enough time a new social equilibrium on this matter may arise, this may entail a long period of disagreement and moral disorder.
(2) The rules of social morality can conflict. Again, although some rules of priority are no doubt part of social morality (we usually know what to do when a promise conflicts with saving a life), many of these conflicts may be unresolved by social morality, and so a more formal system of adjudication may be required.
(3) The informal punishments of social morality may be insufficient to enforce moral rules when the temptations to cheat are high.
(4) Our social order may be stuck at a social equilibrium outside the socially eligible set – that is, we may have an oppressive social morality that some free and equal moral persons do not have reason to endorse and abide by.

An agency that protects, sustains, and develops our social morality is justified by our very devotion to social morality conjoined with the knowledge that problems (1) to (4) are endemic features of life – at least in large-scale modern societies.

Recall that Simmons is ready to accept the Kantian claim that states are justified: what he challenges is that this type of justification implies a political obligation to obey (§1). Note, though, that when states are justified as harmonizers and developers of social morality, this justification implies that the judgments of the state articulate social morality, which is authoritative and obligatory. Insofar as the task of the state is to, as it were, continue on with the development of social morality by political means, when it fulfills these tasks it imposes obligations via the authority of social morality. The social contract tradition was wrong in holding that a political umpire or adjudicator is always a necessary, constitutive, element of justice among individuals (§2.1), but it was correct that in many instances it is necessary. And this necessity is not simply an instrumental necessity: the state's actions as developer of social morality is constitutive of some of our moral relations with others (§2.1). Social morality both constrains the state (where we have a social equilibrium on a member of the eligible set, the demands of morality are clear) and yet it is also completed by the state, when it provides the means for adopting a member of the eligible set.

The role of social consent

The state is morally justified if (1) it is required to protect, sustain, and develop social morality. We also should add that for any particular state to be justified it must (2) be within the socially eligible set of all institutional structures that fulfill the role specified in (1). For a state T to have moral authority qua sustainer and developer of social morality, both conditions must be met. Again, we have arrived at an eligible set that is not a singleton. Members of G^* would almost certainly be unable to settle on a uniquely best regime. Although some form of democracy, understood as a representative system with rights of participation and political pluralism, is surely abstractly justified, members of G^* will not concur on which system is best. Democracies differ in fundamental ways: whether they are majoritarian or consensual, unicameral or bicameral, whether they are proportional representation, are parliamentary or presidential, have a unitary of federal structure, possess a written or an unwritten constitution, have a strong or weak system of judicial review – just to name some of the more obvious factors. Members of G^* will have reasonable differences about how to rank different democratic regimes. Whether we take these issues as a bundle (members of G^* choose regimes types), or divide them up into a series of choices, members of G^* will order the options differently.

As with social morality itself, different societies arrive at different equilibria on these matters, largely on the basis of a path-dependent political history. Just as the justification of the rules of social morality from the impartial deliberative perspective of the commonwealth of ends (G^*) is insufficient to yield a determinate publicly justified social morality, so too is the abstract justification of democracy and its attendant political rights insufficient to yield the justification of a system of governance. Public reason does not mandate a specific democratic regime (how could it?). To be sure, those committed to a democracy that secures publicly justified outcomes may well advance proposals for institutional design that, in their view, do a better job than other arrangements, but rational and good-willed individuals will disagree about the merits of these proposals. Political authority too relies on informal social authority – an evolution of a political culture leading to the selection of one of a wide range of acceptable political systems.

Understood as an institutional system that is required to protect, sustain, and develop social morality (and its rights), the authority of an existing, justified state, and the corresponding obligation of its citizens to obey, is indeed based on the consent of the governed. For the state thus understood is itself a development of social morality, and so like all social morality it is the result of numerous individual choices over a long process that leads to a the specific social equilibrium. Again, this is not a collective 'we choice' that we make together, or a one-time social contract or constitutional convention. It is an ongoing social choice, arrived at by a path-dependent history, and continually reaffirmed by the choices of its members. Filmer (1991, p. 142) was correct:

> Mankind is like a sea, ever ebbing or flowing, every minute one is born and another dies. Those that are the people this minute, are not the people the next minute. In every instant and point of time there is variation.

But this does not preclude the important idea that political authority rests on the ongoing consent of the governed.

The arbitrary will and the power of promising

The social contract's reliance on consent seems to invoke consent qua promising: one is bound to obey the terms of the contract (to obey the law) because one has promised to do so. I have been at pains to show that consent need not be in the form of a promise. The members of the socially eligible set are *justified* authoritative rules or institutions; a society exercises real *choice* in deciding on which of these they shall equilibrate. No promise, explicit or tacit, is involved. But can promises truly bind, and could they form the basis of political obligation?

Some doubt that actual consent, even if it could be obtained, would yield true political obligations (Gilbert 2006, pp. 75–83, Estlund 2008, pp. 49–50). The actual consent view seems to allow that one can be bound just because no one has yet thought of the decisive problem with an institution; once it occurs to someone and she withdraws her consent, then the institution immediately is delegitimized. It would seem that actual consent cannot provide the basis for assured continuing obligations – there is, we might say, justificatory instability. Now relying on consent qua promising avoids this problem: to promise is not just to agree for now, but to bind oneself. Even if it later occurs to you after the promise that perhaps it was not such a great idea to promise, you are, generally, nevertheless bound. On Hobbes, 1994, p. 85) view of promising and contract, unless a crucial new piece of information becomes available between the time of promising and the time of performance, one is bound to perform, regardless of second thoughts.

This response to the problem of justificatory instability seems simply to lead to a deeper problem, stressed by Hegel (1952, p. 157) who charged that Rousseau's general will, being based on actual and not rational wills, therefore founds the state on citizens' 'arbitrary wills,' and 'and their capriciously given consent.' Hegel is entirely right that a fundamental aspect of promissory obligations is our moral power to bind our future action to our present 'arbitrary wills.' Many find this power mysterious, and seek to base promising on more fundamental, and non-arbitrary, moral principles (e.g., Scanlon 1998, ch. 7). I believe this is a mistake. One of the most basic features of moral agency, especially in a diverse society in which people fundamentally disagree about values, ends, and moral ideals, is the ability of individuals to, as it were, extend the bounds of morality through their individual choices and agreements. A framework of common moral rules is necessary for ordered moral relations, but insufficient. We not only need to invoke the common authority of social morality in our relations with strangers, but we need specialized moral claims with respect to those with whom we share ends and ideals. One way – though not the only way – to extend moral obligations is through our distinctive moral power as agents to create moral obligations through promising. Just as a distinctive legal power of a legislature is to create obligations, a distinctive self-legislative power of a free and equal moral person is to create obligations on herself. This power follows from our very status of self-legislative agents. In terms of the categories I have employed, it is not our legislative power qua members of G^* (in Hegel's terms, our rational wills), but our legislative power simply as members of G (our actual, arbitrary, wills) that legislate promise-based morality.

An effective social morality needs to respect the self-legislation of arbitrary, actual, wills. We can say some things about what members of G^* would endorse, but this is, I have argued, surprising modest. Often it is simply unclear what a person has reasons to endorse – what his G^* counterpart would agree to. A person's reasons are complex, and his deliberations are often inconclusive. As an actual agent in the world, he must often act on his own, often incomplete and imperfect, deliberations about what he has reason to do. Fundamental to being an actual agent is to have the authority to decide in these sorts of cases what one has reason to do. If I had deliberated on your beliefs and values, I would have decided that ϕ is the thing to do, but you deliberate and decide that γ is. This is not simply a disagreement, in which we both have competing claims. That you have decided γ rather than ϕ is normally decisive: to be an agent is to be guided by your deliberations about what you should do, even if from an impartial epistemic point of view, my decision is superior. In Hegelian terms, actual agents are typically guided by their actual, even if arbitrary, wills. Because a purely rational morality is impossible (or, at least, we have no idea what it would be), real moralities must respect our arbitrary wills and, indeed, must allow that our moral self-legislation is often based on them. Our power to bind by promising is perhaps the most important way this is accomplished in our social morality.

The problem, then, is not that arbitrary wills cannot morally bind themselves. The real difficulties for the promissory view of political obligations are two. The first is recognized by all: it is simply implausible to think that many have bound themselves in this way to any state, so obligation through promise is never a plausible ground for a case that there is an obligation of almost all citizens to obey the law, just because it is the law. However, even if that obvious – and as far as I can see insurmountable – difficulty could be overcome, an account of political obligation based solely on promissory obligations would remain objectionable. Hegel was basically correct: to base obligations *simply* on the arbitrary wills of a group of people is insufficient to assure us that our basic framework is not unjust and irrational. If all happen agree we may leave well enough alone, but the worry lingers: is the entire framework based on errors, superstitions, and the effects of social indoctrination? Unless we are convinced that the foundations of the framework are set in good reasons that all can endorse, the worry gnaws that our moral and political lives are nothing but an arbitrary, perhaps oppressive, social equilibrium.

Conclusion: consent theory as devices of reconciliation

I have stressed in this paper how the authority of social morality and political obligation are the result of a complex interplay of our rational and actual wills, or what we might think of as hypothetical and actual consent. Arguments from the hypothetical consent focus on an idealized group G^*, seeking to showing what authoritative rules and institutions all members of G have reasons to endorse. As Kant stressed, until we have common rules that reflect public reason, there simply is no public justice: we have only different people employing their private reason, each asserting what he thinks justice is. But, as I have stressed, to respect others as free and equal is inconsistent with claiming such authority of one's private reason over them. Only rules endorsed by public reason can reconcile authority with our status as free and equal. However the reasoning from this perspective (that of G^*) is indeterminate: in a diverse society no single moral rule over any area of social life is endorsed by public reason. Here, I have argued social morality employs a second device of reconciliation: a social choice of one member of the eligible set on which we coordinate. This is a real choice. In Hegelian terms, we might say that it is based on partly on our rational, and partly on our joint arbitrary wills. Insofar as we are rational, we restrict our choice to the socially eligible set; but within that set a society chooses via the interaction of its members' arbitrary wills, producing a social equilibrium. Lastly, I have argued that the device of promising grants each free and equal person the moral power to employ her arbitrary will to grant others moral authority over her. It allows self-legislation by actual free and equal moral persons, based on their full set of ideals, values, and ends.

The consent tradition and liberalism developed together. Liberalism's devotion to the moral freedom and equality of all can only be reconciled with moral and political authority though forms of consent – all of which are exercises of self-legislation, some rational, some quite arbitrary. The problem has been the insistence that one form of consent is the unique device of reconciliation. Different aspects of the consent tradition perform some tasks of reconciliation well, but all are implausible when pressed as the sole method of reconciliation. Once we appreciate that 'consent theory' is not a foundational commitment, but an array of devices for reconciling our status as free and equal with relations of authority, we can stop battling about which is correct and investigate what tasks each can perform.

Notes

1. We should not think that even Rawls holds that the justification of principles of justice can simply ignore the issues about which we disagree. Although the free-standing argument from the original position is based simply on shared models of the person, Rawls (1996, p. 386) insists that this is a 'pro tanto' or 'as far as it goes' justification. What he calls 'full justification' requires that the principles of justice be evaluated in light of one's entire conception of value.
2. It is important to stress that 'utility' is a mathematical representation of an agent's judgement as to how well a rule satisfies her values, aims, and moral ideals. It is not either itself a unique value (such as welfare), or a goal to be pursued.
3. Again, we should not be misled by the language of 'preference.' To prefer R_A to R_B is simply to rank R_A over R_B for purposes of choice; in our terms, one's evaluative standards indicate reason to rank R_A over R_B – this is all that is implied by saying one has a preference for R_A over R_B.
4. The path-breaking work on increasing returns was done by W. Brian Arthur (Arthur 1994). For the technically minded, this convergence can be analyzed in terms of positive network externalities.
5. It is important to distinguish this notion of consent from promissory obligations, which I consider below. Compare Gilbert (2006, p. 55): 'Actual consent theory invokes an agreement as opposed to a contract in law.'

References

Arthur, W. B., 1994. *Increasing returns and path dependency in the economy.* Ann Arbor, MI: University of Michigan Press.
Baier, K., 1965. *The moral point of view.* New York, NY: Random House.
Bicchieri, C., 2006. *The grammar of society: the nature and dynamics of norms.* Cambridge: Cambridge University Press.
Boyd, R. and Richerson, P., 2005. *The origin and evolution of culture.* Oxford: Oxford University Press.
Darwall, S., 2006. *The second-person standpoint: morality, respect and accountability.* Cambridge, MA: Harvard University Press.
Estlund, D., 2008. *Democratic authority.* Princeton, NJ: Princeton University Press.
Filmer, R., 1991. *Patriarcha. In: Patriarcha and other writings.* Cambridge: Cambridge University Press, 1–68.
Freidman, D., 2008. *Morals and markets: an evolutionary account of the modern world.* New York, NY: Palgrave Macmillan.
Gaus, G., 2011a. *The order of public reason: a theory of freedom and morality in a diverse and bounded world.* Cambridge: Cambridge University Press.
Gaus, G., 2011b. The property equilibrium in our liberal social order. *Social Philosophy and Policy*, 28 (2), 74–101.
Gilbert, M., 2006. *A theory of political obligation.* Oxford: Clarendon.
Green, T. H., 1986. Lectures on the principles of political obligation. *In: Lectures on the principles of political obligation and other writings.* Cambridge: Cambridge University Press, 13–193.
Hegel, G. W. F., 1952. *The philosophy of right.* Oxford: Oxford University Press.
Hobbes, T., 1994. *Leviathan.* Indianapolis, IN: Hackett.
Kant, I., 1999. *The metaphysical elements of justice.* 2nd edition Indianapolis: Hackett.
Locke, J., 1960. *The second treatise of government* in *two treatises of government.* Cambridge: Cambridge University Press.
Martin, R., 1993. *A system of rights.* Oxford: Clarendon.
Nagel, T., 1991. *Equality and partiality.* New York, NY: Oxford University Press.
Rawls, J., 1996. *Political liberalism.* New York, NY: Columbia University Press.
Rawls, J., 1999. *A theory of justice.* Cambridge, MA: Harvard University Press.
Richerson, P. J. and Boyd, R., 2008. The evolution of free enterprise values. *In*: P. Zak, ed. *Moral markets: the critical role of values in the economy.* Princeton, NJ: Princeton University Press, 107–141.
Scanlon, T. M., 1998. *What we owe each other.* Cambridge, MA: Belknap.
Schwab, D. and Ostrom, E., 2008. The vital role of norms and rules in maintaining open public and private economies. *In*: P. Zak, ed. *Moral markets: the critical role of values in the economy.* Princeton, NJ: Princeton University Press, 204–27.
Simmons, A. J., 2001. *Justification and legitimacy: essays on rights and obligations.* Cambridge: Cambridge University Press.

Political legitimacy, justice and consent

John Horton

Politics, International Relations and Philosophy, Keele University, Keele, UK

What is it for a state, constitution or set of governmental institutions to have political legitimacy? This paper raises some doubts about two broadly liberal answers to this question, which can be labelled 'Kantian' and 'libertarian'. The argument focuses in particular on the relationship between legitimacy and principles of justice and on the place of consent. By contrast with these views, I suggest that, without endorsing the kind of voluntarist theory, according to which political legitimacy is simply created by individual consent, an adequate understanding of political legitimacy should take much more account than most philosophical theories tend to do of the attitudes and beliefs of citizens and the social and political context in which they have saliency. This also involves acknowledging the limits of theory in determining criteria of political legitimacy.

What is it for a state, constitution or set of governmental institutions to have legitimacy? Why does this question matter and how should we go about answering it? How does political legitimacy relate to whether or not a state or set of political arrangements is just or whether or not we consented to it?[1] It is this cluster of questions on which I focus in this article. In doing so, I do not propose anything as ambitious as to try to answer them all, or even to set out anything remotely approaching a comprehensive theory of political legitimacy. Indeed, as may become apparent, I am somewhat sceptical about the possibility of a compelling substantive normative *theory* of political legitimacy of the kind to which many philosophers and political theorists have aspired; but I do not make a serious effort to defend that claim here. Rather, more specifically, I want, first, to raise a few doubts about two broadly liberal interpretations of a particular idea of political legitimacy, which I label 'Kantian' and 'libertarian', although these are merely labels and no significance should be attached their appropriateness or otherwise. As part of this discussion, I give particular attention to the case for decoupling legitimacy from justice and to the place of consent. Finally, I shall make a few more positive comments about how we might think about political legitimacy, although without claiming to have resolved the many the difficulties to which the idea of political legitimacy gives rise. Probably the most controversial claim I want to defend in this regard is that an adequate understanding of political legitimacy should take much more account than most philosophical theories tend to do of the attitudes and beliefs of citizens and their social and political context. But, as I shall explain, this does not mean that we must revert to endorsing a voluntarist theory of political legitimacy. Moreover, I shall also try to articulate this view in a way that is not open to a standard objection to the Weberian account of legitimacy; the claim that it is unacceptably reductivist (Beetham 1991, pp. 11-12). It should be acknowledged from the start, however, that what is presented remains no more than a highly tentative and preliminary sketch of an alternative approach to theorizing political legitimacy.

I

We need to begin, though, by saying something about why legitimacy matters and how it figures in our thinking about the state and political institutions. A helpful statement of what is involved in the idea of legitimacy and the role that it plays in our thoughts about how we stand in relation to the state is provided by David Copp when writes:

> When we evaluate a state for its legitimacy, our concern is to assess its moral authority to govern. The laws of a state require or prohibit us to act in certain ways, and the state typically enforces its law by attaching punishments or penalties to failures to comply. Criminal law is only one example, and it is not a typical example, since unlike other parts of the law, much of the criminal law requires actions or forbearances that would be morally required in any event. In other parts of the law, such as the traffic code, some actions that are legally required would not be morally required in the absence of the law. In all of these cases, there is the problem of explaining by what right the state imposes requirements and by what right it enforces them. … The problem of legitimacy is, then, to explain how a state can have the moral authority to do the kinds of thing involved in governing. (Copp 1999, pp. 4-5)

In short, the role of an account of political legitimacy is to explain how it is that a state has the right or, as I shall say, the *authority* to govern those who are subject to it. Legitimacy determines who has political authority, by virtue of what characteristics, qualities or processes it is possessed, and also what those who have political authority may properly to do. Moreover, it follows that if a law or policy is enacted by a legitimate political authority, those subject to it are afforded good, though not necessarily decisive, reasons to comply with its directives.

Without legitimacy, a state, in so far as it can, may be able to exercise coercive power effectively, but this amounts to no more than one collection of people, through force, deception or some other means, being able to get another collection of people to do as it wishes. That is not legitimate governance, and the effectiveness of such power does not, simply of itself, confer legitimacy on those who exercise it: might does not make right. Indeed, it has been argued by Bernard Williams that this latter state of affairs scarcely counts as a political relationship at all.

> The situation of one lot of people terrorizing another lot of people is not per se a political situation: it is, rather, the situation which the existence of the political is in the first place supposed to alleviate (replace). If the power of one lot of people over another is to represent a solution to the first political question [the problem of achieving and maintaining order], and not itself be part of the problem, *something* has to be said to explain (to the less empowered, to concerned bystanders, to children being educated in this structure, etc.) what the difference is between the solution and the problem, and that cannot simply be an account of successful domination.
>
> (Williams 2005, p. 5)

It is this, apparently fairly minimal, idea that there should be an acknowledgement that something needs to be said by those who exercise state power to those who are subject to it, and which amounts to more than just the assertion that because the former can coerce the latter they will, which lies at the heart of the idea of political legitimacy. It is what Williams calls 'the basic legitimation demand' (pp. 3-5), and any account of political authority must be responsive to it. This does not determine any specific content to what need to be said, and it is quite consistent with judgements about what is sufficient being a matter of dispute: the claim to political legitimacy may not always be settled or uncontested, but all parties that claim a relationship of *political authority*, rather than one of mere domination, must recognize the basic legitimation demand as something that needs to be addressed.

It is not surprising, therefore, that the question of legitimacy has been at the centre of political theory for much of its history; Robert Nozick, for instance, calls it 'the fundamental question' of political philosophy (Nozick 1974, p. 4). Historically, of course, a number of different answers have been given to the question, including the answer that there is no answer, and thus that states do not have any political authority over those they govern. That is, not just this or that state, but all states are illegitimate. This is the view of pretty much all anarchists; including the so-called 'philosophical anarchism' of Robert Paul Wolff (Wolff 1976), and in effect A. J. Simmons, to whom I shall be returning later (Simmons 1979, 2001, ch. 6). Others, like Nozick, have thought that it may be possible, in principle, to explain the legitimacy of the state, but only if the state limits itself to a far narrower range of activities than any existing states undertake.[2] And there have also been a wide range of attempts to show that much more than a minimal state can be legitimate. Some of the most interesting of these attempts have arisen from within the classical social contract tradition of Hobbes, Locke and Rousseau. One especially philosophically sophisticated strand within that broad tradition, ultimately often traced to Kant, continues to have considerable attraction, particularly to liberals, and it is on this view that I initially want to focus.

II

One influential interpretation of something like Williams's basic legitimation demand, which is claimed to lie at the heart of liberal political theory, and sometimes labelled 'Kantian', has been articulated by Jeremy Waldron:[3]

> I want to present liberalism as, at bottom, a theory about what makes political action – and in particular the enforcement and maintenance of a social and political order – morally legitimate. The thesis that I want to say is *fundamentally* liberal is this: a social and political order is illegitimate unless it is rooted in the consent of all those who have to live under it; and the consent or agreement of these people is a condition of its being morally permissible to enforce that order against them. (Waldron 1993, p. 50)

However, this apparently straightforward statement of the ideal of liberal legitimacy is potentially misleading if one takes at face value the idea that people must actually consent to political arrangements for them to be legitimate. For a few lines later Waldron glosses this view as follows: 'Understood in this way, the liberal position provides a basis for arguing against some arrangement or institution inasmuch as one can show that it has not secured, *or perhaps could not secure* [added emphasis], the consent of the people' (Waldron 1993, p. 50). And only a couple of pages later there is no longer any 'perhaps' about it, and the condition of liberal legitimacy has become: 'not whether the individuals who live in it have agreed to its terms, but whether its terms *can be represented* [added emphasis], as the object of an agreement between them' (p. 53). Thus, it is the claim that, in some relevant sense, it *could* have been the object of an agreement between citizens – a position sometimes presented in terms of a 'hypothetical contract' – that makes a state or political order legitimate.

So, Waldron moves quickly from a principle of legitimacy that initially appeared to depend upon people actually agreeing or consenting to the political arrangements under which they live to one in which legitimacy depends instead on the possibility that the political order can be represented as being the object of their agreement or consent, whether or not they have, or would have in fact, agreed or consented. Thus, in its final formulation, the principle of liberal legitimacy, as Waldron understands it, says something like: political institutions are legitimate only in so far as they could in principle be agreed by each and every person who is subject to them. Thomas Nagel elaborates what is basically the same ideal, when he writes:

> The search for legitimacy is a search for unanimity – not about everything but about the controlling framework within which more controversial decisions will be made. The unanimity in question is neither actual unanimity among persons with the motives they happen to have, nor the kind of ideal unanimity that simply follows from there being a single right answer which everyone ought to accept because it is independently right, but rather something in between: a unanimity which could be achieved among persons in many respects as they are, provided they were also reasonable and committed within reason to modifying their claims, requirements and motives in a direction which makes a common framework of justification possible.
> (Nagel 1991, pp. 33-34)

However, although presented by Nagel as the search for a particular kind of unanimity, as he readily concedes, a political order need not in fact be accepted or believed to be justified by those who are subject to it, for it to be legitimate. In this way political legitimacy easily becomes detached from any actual allegiance or support and, in principle at least, it would seem possible on this view that a state could be legitimate even though few, if any, of its citizens actually accept that it is; or could be illegitimate even though all of its citizens endorse it as legitimate. But, whether or not these extreme scenarios are at all likely, one significant theoretical point is the displacement of actual consent by a supposedly justified form of hypothetical consent; one which is through and through a theoretical construction.

This shift away from actual consent is not, of course, inadvertent or unacknowledged. Waldron explicitly draws attention to one of its most important implications in writing that

> when we move from asking people what they accept to asking what they *would* accept under certain conditions, we shift our emphasis away from the will and focus on the *reasons* that people might have for exercising their will in one way rather than another. (Waldron 1993, p. 55)

That is, what is important on this account of political legitimacy is, ultimately, not any volitional act by citizens but the kind of reasons available to them for accepting the authority of a state. In enquiring as to whether a political regime is legitimate, therefore, on this view, we should turn not to social scientists (or market researchers) to establish whether or not it has the actual support of its citizens, but instead seek to assess the normative validity of the kinds of reasons that would justify its support, whether or not it is in fact supported. And this task is taken to be the province of normative political theorists and philosophers. On the Kantian view, what matters is the quality of reasons, not what people in fact believe or think about the legitimacy of their state. As has been seen, we are no longer interested, at least from the point of view of giving of an account of political legitimacy, in whether citizens do consent or in what they actually endorse, which tends pretty much to drop out of the picture, but in what they should believe – about what is normatively justifiable, a question to which people's own views about the legitimacy of their state are taken to be of no particular relevance.

While the details of what can be normatively justified differ between liberal theorists, the form or shape of what is needed is pretty uniform. For what we might think of as this kind of liberal's philosopher's stone is the

> search for underlying interests and beliefs shared in common which may be appealed to in the justification of our institutional arrangements: the basic needs of nature, certain desired objects that are means to the pursuit of any ideal, common general beliefs about how the world works, similar modes of argument and reason, and so on. (Waldron 1993, p. 56)

And for all their acknowledgement of the value of diversity and need to permit it to flourish, as Waldron also acutely observes, this implies that:

> all ethical commitment has a common form: that there is something like *pursuing a conception of the good life* that all people, even those with the most diverse commitments, can be said to be engaged in. … The hunch is that, although people do not share one another's ideals, they can at least abstract from their experience a sense of *what it is like to be committed to an ideal of the good life*; they can recognize this in others and they can focus on it as something to which political justification ought to be addressed. (Waldron 1993, p. 56)

So, although not all of them would want to formulate their views in quite this way, such liberals see political legitimacy as depending upon finding a way to justify a particular political order to its citizens who, although they have diverse ideals and beliefs, still have good reasons to comply with it, whatever else they (reasonably) believe. And this, in essence, has been *the* project of a swathe of Rawlsian and post-Rawlsian liberal political theorists (which is not to suggest that a similar quest cannot be found much earlier than Rawls).

This is not the place for a general critical exploration of the different ways in which this project has been executed.[4] Instead, I want to point to how this approach to political legitimacy has tended to become closely bound up with another one: the search for a theory of justice. Within this vein of liberal theory, and simplifying somewhat, justice becomes in essence a condition of its legitimacy. Interestingly, Waldron often moves apparently unreflectively between the two concepts, sometimes writing of justice and sometimes of legitimacy without there seeming to be for him any distinction of significance between them. In *A Theory of Justice* Rawls's account of political legitimacy is in substance underpinned by his theory of justice.[5] Even Samuel Freeman, who stresses more than most the distinction between legitimacy and justice in Rawls's work, says of his principle of liberal legitimacy that 'implicit in it is a requirement of basic justice' (Freeman 2007a, p. 376). For, although Rawls does indeed argue in *A Theory of Justice* that we sometimes have a duty to comply with individual laws that are (moderately) unjust, this is so only where the constitution of a state is at least 'nearly just' (Rawls 1999, sect. 3). This minimal concession seems only to reflect the fact that even a basically just state cannot reasonably be expected to be free of all unjust laws or institutions. Justice and legitimacy are, however, still very closely connected, with justice grounding and setting the parameters to a state's political legitimacy. And, in many other liberal theories it similarly appears that either justice and legitimacy are more or less conflated, because justice is effectively the criterion of political legitimacy, or legitimacy tracks justice pretty closely, because the account of legitimacy is ultimately parasitic on the account of justice.

Such an account of the relationship between justice and legitimacy is, however, open to question. It is surely perfectly intelligible (and, I suggest, morally defensible) to say, for example, that one believes that the British state is legitimate while also accepting that its basic structure is in some fundamental respects unjust. Let me briefly elaborate on what saying something like that amounts to. First, I am saying that I hold the political institutions – the government, the law, the judiciary etc. - to be authoritative; that the state is entitled to make claims on me that I as, say, a British citizen, along with other British citizens, take to impose obligations on us. That does not mean that I, or British citizens in general, should always, all things considered, act in accordance with the laws or perform other duties that the state requires of us. For one thing, it may act outside its authority, and, for another, even when acting within its authority, there may be conflicting ethical demands that can properly be deemed to be weightier, and thus justify non-compliance. (That a refusal to comply may be quite consistent with acknowledging the authority of the state is a point of fundamental importance if potentially unacceptable implications of how the argument presented here might be interpreted are to be avoided.[6]) However, the possibility that particular directives of the state can be overridden by other moral claims does not mean that one should comply with state authority only if one happens to agree with what it demands – the state's being authoritative supplies an independent reason for complying; just not necessarily a decisive one.

Secondly, in saying that Britain is in some respects deeply unjust, I may refer to fundamental features of its basic structure. An example of such a feature might be the massive and unjustified (as I see it) inequalities in the distribution of wealth. Of course, my view of a just distribution of wealth can be challenged – in fact I do not have a clear view of what a just distribution would be, but that is another story – but I do have a clear idea that some distributions are *unjust*, and that the distribution of wealth in contemporary Britain indubitably falls within the category of the unjust. Indeed, levels of inequality are not merely unjust, in the sense that they are not ideally just, but are fundamentally unjust, even iniquitous, and have far reaching social and political consequences, including serious implications for the value of some basic liberties. (This is also what Rawls's theory of justice would seem tell us, although Rawls is not always as clear as he might be what constitutes an unjust society, beyond some rather obvious and flagrant examples.) In short, Britain is in important respects, at least in my view, not even 'nearly just'. The point, though, is not whether one agrees with the substantive judgement about the injustice of the levels of inequality in Britain. Rather, it is whether it is intelligible and defensible to hold such a view about political institutions being legitimate but fundamentally unjust. If it is, and such views are surely not at all uncommon, then the political legitimacy of a state cannot be at all closely tied to the extent to which it instantiates or tracks some particular, preferred principles of justice.[7]

One reason why this matters is that according to almost all currently philosophically favoured theories of justice, virtually all states, both now and in the past, are and have always been unjust. Nor are they, if one is honest about it, even 'almost just'. But, if this is so, the question we are left with is: where do we stand in relation to states that are unjust? And in particular, and rather pressingly, where do we stand in relation to the existing unjust states of which we are members? For, if legitimacy at all closely tracks justice, it seems we must also infer that they lack legitimacy. If they lack legitimacy then I take it that they *ipso facto* lack political authority over us; or at most they only have authority in those areas where they are acting justly or nearly justly. But this account of how we stand in relation to unjust states of which we are members, however, seems to me to be seriously inadequate. It leaves us in a necessarily indeterminate relation to our state and unclear what we are supposed to think of our relationship to it. Moreover, if one is exercised by the apparent illegitimacy of virtually all states, one potential danger in linking so closely justice and legitimacy is that in order to avoid this problem we may be tempted to claim that some states are more just than we truly believe them to be. So, another reason for decoupling justice and legitimacy is that it makes it easier to resist this temptation; because, in criticizing our state and its political institutions as in important respects fundamentally unjust, we can still accept that they have legitimate authority over us. This decoupling opens up a space for the criticism of political institutions as unjust without also having to commit oneself to the view that they therefore lack political legitimacy. Precisely because legitimacy does not track justice at all closely, we can vigorously criticize our political institutions in terms of justice (and other ideals) without undermining their political authority. In this respect, the delinking of legitimacy and injustice can be seen to be good both for justice and for political legitimacy.

III

Before proceeding to what I intend to propose as a better approach to understanding political legitimacy, I want to turn to a different interpretation of the liberal principle of legitimacy. This alternative view takes more seriously the initial idea that if a state is to have political legitimacy it requires the actual consent of those who live under it. It endorses some of the doubts that I have expressed about the preceding, Kantian account; however, it does so from a very different perspective and comes to a radically different conclusion. Those who adopt this approach, which might loosely be labelled 'libertarian', criticize the view we have just been considering on the grounds that, ultimately, it is not committed to the voluntary principle at all. Thus, one of the most tenacious advocates of this approach, Simmons, argues that the Kantian view seems to rest on the thought that:

> The idea of a fully voluntary society should of course guide us, but the (regrettable) facts of political life force us instead to accept nonvoluntarist standards of legitimacy which appeal only to … 'quasi-voluntariness'. There is, though, something disingenuous about this suggestion. For if the ideal of the fully voluntary political society were in any way regulative for them, Rawls (et al) would be interested in restructuring political societies so as to make the choice of membership (or nonmembership) as voluntary at least as circumstances would permit. … Few of the most prominent contemporary political philosophers, however, have shown any interest in such matters, suggesting that any allegiance they might feel to the voluntarist ideal is at best half-hearted. (Simmons 2001, pp. 146-147)

He goes on to claim that such theorists 'have illicitly appropriated the justificatory force of voluntarism while being (like Kant) in no real way motivated by it' (Simmons 2001, p. 147). As noted above in discussing Waldron's account of the principle of liberal legitimacy, there is a fundamental shift away from the question of whether citizens have consented, or whether they would in fact consent, to the questions about whether they should consent, whether they have good reasons to consent; and the latter, as Simmons rightly says, 'have a very different moral basis and force than do appeals to actual choice' (Simmons 2001, p. 147). In short, having a good reason to agree or consent to something is not at all the same as actually doing so.

According to Simmons, the problem is that the theorists he is criticizing have confused the question of whether the state is justified with whether it is legitimate: these are two different and distinct questions. In particular, showing a state to be justified does not show it to be legitimate. The justification of a state is about 'showing that some realizable type of state is on balance morally permissible (or ideal) and that it is rationally preferable to all feasible nonstate alternatives' (Simmons 2001, p. 126). On the other hand, a state's legitimacy resides in

> its exclusive right to impose new duties on its subjects by initiating legally binding directives, to have those directives obeyed, and to coerce noncompliers. This right and its correlative obligations constitute a particular moral relationship between that particular state and each particular (consenting) subject. (p. 137)

Simmons is making two points here. First, that legitimacy involves a special relationship between the state and its citizens that is not *ipso facto* established by showing a state to be justified. Indeed, Simmons claims that 'none of [their] reasons, quite plausibly offered in support of having states, translates naturally into a reason why any particular contemporary person must become or remain a member of some state' (p. 152). His second point is that the only justifiable basis for such a relationship, and therefore the only basis for attributing legitimacy to states, is one of consent.[8] But, it is important to note that these are two separate claims; and that the first does not follow from the second.

The, perhaps predictable, sting in the tail of Simmons's argument is that states are not, therefore, generally legitimate because, with a few possible exceptions, people have not voluntarily consented to join or be members or to their authority. Nor is at all easy to see how the conditions for genuine voluntary consent could obtain in the modern world: it seems wholly implausible to think that the world can be so arranged that everyone has a genuine, voluntary choice about whether or not to consent to membership or the authority of their state.[9] The problems with basing the authority of the state on an actual act of consent by its citizens have been extensively rehearsed in the context of consent theories of political obligation, and there is no need to dwell further on them here (Horton 2010a, ch. 2). As a result, Simmons ends up in one respect in a position that is actually quite close to that I attributed to the Kantian liberal, because on neither account is there a satisfactory basis for attributing political legitimacy to (almost) any actual states. The difference is that whereas this is not the conclusion that the Kantian liberals were explicitly arguing for, and is indeed one that would be unwelcome to most of them, Simmons, by contrast, is entirely comfortable with it, and happily embraces the claim that all modern states, for example, are illegitimate.

One of the major problems with Simmons's argument, however, is its 'libertarian' starting point, or what I shall call its background picture. This is one in which we begin by assuming the absence of a state or any political community at all, and then seek to show how, in principle at least, it could be rendered legitimate. Moreover, if it turns out that the only thing that can render it legitimate is some voluntary act by those who are to be subject its authority then, I suggest, it is an approach that is inevitably doomed to failure, at least if one is hoping to arrive at a plausible justification of the legitimacy of any actual states. For I think that there is certainly this much to be said in favour of Simmons's argument: if the challenge of accounting for political legitimacy is set up against the background that he assumes, there is little prospect of the challenge being successfully met, and the pull of something like philosophical anarchism becomes hard to resist. By contrast, however, I think that this should lead us not to embrace philosophical anarchism but to question whether the background picture is the appropriate place to begin; whether the invitation to seek a justification of political legitimacy in the terms that Simmons presents it is one that we should be accept. Rather, in my view, a philosophical account of political legitimacy should seek to explain how political legitimacy is possible – not in some world that never has been and probably never could be, but in our world. Naturally, there can never be any guarantee in advance that we can come up with such an explanation. It may simply be that we are so hopelessly confused about the whole idea of political legitimacy and the way we use it that no convincing sense can be made of it. Such a conclusion, though, would be so serious in its implications that it is not one that we should come to at all lightly. It is, rather, a conclusion that we have strong reasons to wish to avoid, so that we should only accept it if there really is no other plausible option. However, I do not believe that this is the only viable option; and what sets us off in the wrong direction is, I suggest, the background picture that underpins Simmon's whole approach.

There may be nothing that is 'natural' specifically about the state, which is but one form of political organization, and throughout history people have lived in political communities that could not properly be described as states. Wherever people have flourished and prospered for any length of time, though, they have lived in political communities of one sort or other, which has inevitably involved what, in its broadest meaning, would count as political relations. Aristotle was right to claim that a human being is a *zoon politicon*, a political animal. (And, similarly, Rousseau was wrong to think that we are all born free but everywhere are in chains.) In normal circumstances we do not in fact begin life outside of a political community, and it virtually always makes a worthwhile life, whatever that is taken to be, extremely difficult if we have to live for long outside of one (which is not to deny that some political communities are also very unpleasant for those who have to live in them); and even if we grant, as we must, that it is quite possible to conceive of ourselves outside of the particular political community of which we happen to be members, this amounts almost invariably to imagining ourselves as members of some other political community, not conceiving ourselves as entirely outside of any political community whatsoever.[10] There is, therefore, a perfectly straightforward and unobjectionable sense in which we can describe living in a political society as 'natural'; and by this I mean no more than that we know of no viable long-term way in which human beings in general can live valuable and worthwhile lives, whatever exactly a worthwhile life is taken to be, outside of a political society. And even political communities that by some moral standards leave a good deal to be desired, even substantially unjust, are usually preferable to the absence of any political authority. It seems to me, therefore, that the idea that every (realistic) political community is illegitimate is not something that can be seriously entertained.[11] In short, the picture we should begin with is of a person already situated or embedded within a political community, and a political community that will in truth likely be quite seriously deficient by some standards of moral appraisal. We should not, therefore, start with a conveniently socialized but pre-political individual; not least, although not only, because the normal course of socialization is inextricably intertwined with membership of a political community.

Needless to say, this does not imply that any and every political community is necessarily legitimate. I have already alluded to the fact, and should perhaps make it explicit, that political societies can be pretty terrible places for their members. However, given that many political societies, imperfect as they undoubtedly are, do make it possible for their members to live valuable and worthwhile lives, however these are understood, this at least makes them *prima facie* candidates for legitimacy. Ultimately, though, I think that this is only a necessary and not a sufficient condition of any particular political community's being legitimate. For, as I shall shortly suggest, there is also an important role in explaining political legitimacy for the beliefs and attitudes of its members and the broader context in which these are shaped and have their home.

One final point: it may be noted that I began by talking of the state but have now shifted to talk of political community. Does this mark an illicit move in the argument? I do not think so; but this denial can certainly be contested. Political community (or polity) is the more basic or fundamental category, and the state is but one type of political community. But, unless it can be shown that there is something inherent in any and every state that makes it necessarily an unjustifiable form of political community, there is no reason to think that states are a form of political community that cannot be legitimate. It would, though, be disingenuous to pretend that the view I am dismissing does not have its defenders – most obviously classical anarchists – although, despite their embracing of the title of 'anarchist', this is not in fact the view of philosophical anarchist, like Simmons (and nor of course is it the view of Kantian liberals, who tend to be rather keen on the state, or at least the right kind of state). So far as classical anarchism is concerned, though, the argument will have to be left to another occasion.[12]

IV

What I have sought to argue so far is that the task of giving an adequate account of political legitimacy is likely to be undermined from the start if we either tie it too closely to a theory of justice or begin with the background picture that is deployed by Simmons and within the libertarian view. But, if we dispense with the background picture that informs Simmons's approach and legitimacy is conceived of as largely independent from justice, how instead should we seek to explain it? First, I believe that we have to restore the connection between political legitimacy and the beliefs and attitudes of those subject to it, which has largely fallen into disrepute among political philosophers, partly as a result of dissatisfaction with the Weberian account. The objection to (the standard interpretation of) the Weberian view, which I endorse, 'is that it misrepresents the relationship between legitimacy and people's beliefs', for a state 'is not legitimate because people believe in its legitimacy, but because it can be *justified in terms of* their beliefs' (Beetham 1991, p. 11). Thus, secondly, I want to suggest that a much more prominent role should be afforded to the cultural and conceptual context and belief system within which a people frame their thinking about their government and political institutions. On the view that I want to defend, it is the support or allegiance of its members, their affirmation of it, broadly understood, that sustains the claim of a state (or any form of political community) to political legitimacy. This is not, though, a mere matter of aggregating opinions: it is not simply a matter of popularity or even of agreement with its political institutions or principles, and certainly not with particular laws or policies. Fundamentally, it is about the acknowledgement of state as having authority – recognizing the right of the state to exercise state power by making laws, pursuing policies and enforcing them on its citizens that are the routine business of the state – in terms that are taken to be salient within the context in which such authority is exercised and affirmed.[13]

This may sound as if it is nothing more than a retreat to a version of the kind of consent theory that has just been rejected in discussing Simmons's view. However, although it would not be *completely mistaken* to say that something like consent does indeed play *a* role, it is not a consent theory because 'consent', or 'recognition' or 'acknowledgement' as it might be better termed, is not itself the reason on this account why people accept a state as legitimate. This is also, as just explained, the reason why it is not a Weberian account. Consent does not ground or justify political legitimacy: the basis of legitimacy is not to be found in a voluntary decision that makes it legitimate. Although acknowledgement of its authority by its citizens is a part of the story of what it means for a state to be legitimate, it does not follow that it is the giving of consent that creates its legitimacy. Generalizing and simplifying greatly, according to classical consent theory, where it is given, our consent is the *reason* that we have to acknowledge the authority of the state: I acknowledge its authority *because* I have in some way consented to it. If I have not given my consent then the state does not have any legitimacy, at least so far as I am concerned. The image of the social contract, however metaphorically it is interpreted, is central here. What I am arguing, however, is that this misunderstands the role of consent: it gets things the wrong way around.

Thus, I consent to, or more properly recognize or acknowledge, the state as legitimate, because it meets the salient criteria of legitimacy that are practically operative. I do not acknowledge its legitimacy *because* I have consented to it; not least because if consent is understood to be an act that confers authority on the state I typically will not have consented to it. The affirmation of legitimacy matters, but that affirmation is grounded in something other than that affirmation itself. So, what then explains my acknowledging the legitimacy? This can and does vary; and how it varies will depend in part upon the kinds of consideration that underpin legitimacy in the state of which a person is a member. Thus, in my own case it will be because, entirely mundanely, I recognize the political institutions and laws and as having been properly constituted and enacted, and the current government as the duly elected government of Britain. In doing all this I recognize myself, and am recognized by others, as a member of the British state; that is a British citizen. This is how political legitimacy is established in contemporary Britain. But in other times and in other places it is or has been different. David Hume, in the course of his critique of social contract theory and reflecting on the relation of the people to their king in the England of his time, remarks that: ‘they consent, because they apprehend him to be by birth their lawful sovereign’ (Hume 1987). Peter Winch’s comment on Hume’s remark captures precisely the point I want to endorse:

> Consent does indeed play a role in the relation between citizen and ruler in this case, but it is not the role described by social contract theorist. It is not the *source* of their sense of the ruler’s legitimacy; rather, their recognition of his legitimacy is expressed in the role played by the thought of his royal birth in the way they consent to his rule, and the importance they attach to this is of course rooted in the hereditary institutions which belong to their form of life. (Winch 1991, p. 227)[14]

If one wants to call such recognition or acknowledgement 'consent' then there need not necessarily be any great harm in that; but it will result in a serious misunderstanding if it leads one to think that it is consent that is the ground or reason that explains political legitimacy.

Moreover, lest this be thought to be the kind of view that can be safely consigned to an earlier age, it may be helpful to think for example of the attitude of those people of Tibet who regard the Dali Lama as their legitimate ruler.[15] While the Dalai Lama has extensive support, that support is grounded in something entirely distinct from consent, and in this case that something is neither liberal nor democratic, but a highly complex set of ideas and practices that are integral to how those people understand the basis of political authority in their country. However, that such criteria are those that (most of) the people of Tibet employ in deliberating about political legitimacy is what makes him a putative legitimate political leader. It is important to appreciate, however, that this does not simply 'dissolve legitimacy into belief and opinion', and nor would it be true that just because 'a people holds a belief that existing institutions are "appropriate" or "morally proper", then these institutions are legitimate. That's all there is to it' (Schaar 1969, p. 284). There is the possibility on this account that citizens can be mistaken, for example because they wrongly believe that their state meets their criteria of legitimacy when it does not, and they can also call into question those criteria, which are not of course immutable and unrevisable. The point is that, on this view, people are making *judgements* about political legitimacy, and deploying criteria in making those judgements; they are not simply asserting that a state or ruler is legitimate merely because they say so.

To understand how reasoning about political legitimacy functions, therefore, we have to understand the concrete context of the culture, political institutions and intellectual and moral traditions within which such reasoning occurs; the context in which, say, the idea of the Dalai Lama as a legitimate political ruler makes sense. For, as I hope is clear, I am not for a moment suggesting that it would make sense to think that the Dalai Lama (or anything similar) could have legitimate political authority in, say, contemporary Britain. That makes no sense at all. Only if we are tempted by the thought that what a philosophical account should provide is a set of specific, determinate, universal normative criteria for *deciding* political legitimacy are we inexorably led in that direction. By contrast, what I am suggesting is that one of the things we should look is an account that can genuinely accommodate the possibility that political legitimacy may be based on different criteria in different times and places. Such an account will still incorporate a robust distinction between the naked exercise of power and legitimate rule of the kind that Williams remarked on earlier; and that is where something like consent, or at least something that involves the disposition of the will that political legitimacy implies, comes into the picture.

Understanding the role of people's beliefs and the broader cultural and conceptual context in which they function can, I think, also help to extricate us from the kind of confusion that we often get into when we talk about regimes that are not in any standard sense of the term democratic but yet clearly have the allegiance of the majority of their people. What I have been arguing suggests that we can resist both a tendency to regard all regimes that are supported by the majority of their people as in any very meaningful sense democratic and the inclination to deny that such regimes, unless they are truly democratic, can possibly have political legitimacy. This latter is sometimes reflected, for instance, in a desire to show that in such cases the people must necessarily be duped or suffer from false consciousness. Not that this cannot be the case – history has provided ample evidence to show that there certainly can be deceit and misinformation on a grand scale – but it would need to be demonstrated in each particular case; and there is no good reason to think that it can be demonstrated in all cases where regimes do not, for example, match up to the liberal democratic model, that their claims to political legitimacy must be vitiated simply because of this.

To reiterate, none of what has been argued implies that current or conventional criteria of legitimacy cannot be called into question or that their interpretation cannot be controversial and contested. Such questioning and contestation, though, does not call into doubt the idea of political legitimacy itself, but only what the specific criteria for legitimacy are or whether this particular state at this point in time is legitimate. Often, for example, questions arise about whether or how far current institutions and practices, or even the boundaries of the state, reflect cultural and ideational changes within a political community as to what makes for political legitimacy. That itself can form part of the ongoing political process, as for example with the history of the extension of franchise in most Western countries in the 19th and 20th centuries. For, although there is a tendency to theorize political legitimacy simply as property that a state either possesses or lacks, it also needs to be seen in terms of an ongoing process through which legitimacy is affirmed or denied. What I am most concerned to resist here, though, is any suggestion that because of the centrality in my account of standards of political legitimacy that have currency in a particular time and place, these are set in stone or beyond criticism: that is not an implication of anything that has been said.

This account of political legitimacy also has the merit of being realistic in the sense of accommodating the fact that real states will never be very close to how ideal theory envisages them.[16] While many philosophers will say so much the worse for actual states, I am inclined to say so much the worse for ideal theory, or at least a particular conception of ideal theory.

David Beetham seems to me to be right when he remarks that 'we only have the moral and political principles we do because the world is as it is, and not otherwise' (Beetham 1991, p. 244). A political theory that strays too far from 'the world as it is', is likely to be of little relevance to us. Furthermore, part of being realistic is not usurping to political theory what properly belongs to politics. Too many theories of political legitimacy want not only to explain what it involves but also to set down the theorist's own preferred moral criteria for its justification. By contrast, the account presented here regards that as in large part a political matter, not a theoretical one. This does not, however, mean that the account is purely descriptive. The idea of political legitimacy is inherently normative in that it necessarily implies a distinction between legitimate and illegitimate power. There is space in this account, for example, for people to be mistaken or deluded about the legitimacy of their political institutions. But I do want to resist the idea that it is for political theorists to determine for them the criteria by which people everywhere and anytime should judge whether their political institutions are legitimate.

V

I have sought to argue against two interpretations of the liberal principle of legitimacy, claiming that neither presents an adequate account of political legitimacy. The Kantian interpretation links it too closely with principles of justice and effectively detaches legitimacy from people's actual attitudes towards or beliefs about their state. Simmons's more libertarian interpretation, on the other hand, misunderstands the role of consent in political legitimacy, believing that it is the only valid basis for political legitimacy, and thus effectively making it impossible for any actual state to be legitimate. By contrast, I have suggested that we should locate political legitimacy in relation to the criteria that are operative in particular social, cultural and conceptual contexts, and which inform people's judgements about the legitimacy of their state. This allows for a greater pluralism about political legitimacy than either of the two interpretations of the liberal principle of legitimacy, which also allows for a wider diversity of legitimate political structures and institutions. However, although people's beliefs and attitudes to their state are important in this account, it is neither simply Weberian in its approach nor a view in which political legitimacy is to be explained in terms of whether or not citizens have voluntarily consented to it.

What has been offered here is, of course, no more than a gesture towards a different way of thinking about political legitimacy; a sketch of an alternative, and perhaps more modest, approach to how to theorize it. To a considerable extent, I have been concerned with trying to motivate that approach by showing how it is preferable to the two more familiar theories that I have examined, rather than with doing much to develop the account itself, and it would be idle to pretend that it is without difficulties or obscurities as it stands. Clearly much more detailed work needs to be done in articulating and elaborating this approach, if it is to carry the conviction that I believe it should.

Acknowledgments

Earlier versions of this article were presented at the Political Studies Association Annual Conference and the Manchester Workshops in Political Theory, both held in 2009. I am grateful for the helpful discussion on both occasions. I am particularly grateful for their written comments to Massimo Renzo, Bas van der Vossen, Emanuela Ceva and Enzo Rossi.

Notes

1. Hereafter, I shall mostly refer for convenience simply to the 'state', using it as a proxy for the constitution, political institutions and governmental arrangements of a country generally. Obviously, these may need to be differentiated for some purposes, and it is true that the political legitimacy of one need not necessarily imply the legitimacy in all respects of all the others. However, for the purpose of the argument here I believe that no serious damage is done by not systematically distinguishing these terms.
2. Although exactly what Nozick's hypothetical explanation of a minimal state establishes with regard to the legitimacy of any actual or likely state is, to say the least, a moot point.
3. Nearly all the theorists I go on to discuss claim to be articulating a liberal theory of legitimacy. It is not always clear from these theories whether the liberal principle is supposed to be the only valid principle of political legitimacy or whether there could also be other valid principles. I have tended to treat such accounts of legitimacy as if they were exclusive of others, which is how I believe most of the theorists intend them, but insofar as this not the case the subsequent argument would need to be adapted in places.
4. For a thoroughgoing critique of hypothetical agreement arguments, see Bohman and Richardson (2009).
5. Arguably, Rawls's view of legitimacy in *Political Liberalism* is more complex and subtle. Thus Samuel Freeman writes: 'The problem that Rawls confronts in *Political Liberalism* is not the same as in *A Theory of Justice*. … [H]e is not directly addressing the question of the true or (as he says) most reasonable conception of justice that he addressed in *A Theory of Justice*. Instead, he speaks to the question of the conditions of the *stability* of a liberal constitution and its *political legitimacy* - its authority to make and enforce coercive laws and legitimately use coercive power among citizens who conceive of themselves as free and equal' (Freeman 2007b, p. 229).
6. I have defended this view in relation to political obligation in Horton (2010a).
7. This does not mean that there are *no* common conditions relating to justice that a state must meet to be legitimate, only that justice and legitimacy are largely independent of each other.
8. Elsewhere, Simmons provides extensive arguments against attempts to demonstrate that there are other reasons for attributing political obligations to people, which he sees as the necessary correlate of state legitimacy (Simmons 1979,

and 2001). I have tried to defend my view against these criticisms in Horton (2010a, ch. 6).

9. For a contrary view, see Beran (1987).
10. Hermits at least begin their lives in political communities and feral children lack a distinctively human life. But, even if it is possible to come up with highly unusual exceptions to my claims about the centrality to human beings of living in a political community, they are just that: highly unusual. And although I may be too cavalier here, whatever its merits in other branches of philosophy, I think that idea of a highly unusual, let alone merely constructed, supposed 'counter-example' *refuting* a theory is disastrous for serious work in political philosophy.
11. It might be argued that Simmons's claim that a state could be justified without being legitimate could meet all my concerns. I do not have the space here to show why I think that such a claim is implausible, but I have argued the case at some length in Horton (2010a, chs 5, 8).
12. I have engaged with the classical anarchist arguments against political obligation in Horton (2010a, ch. 5).
13. While contestation about some of the criteria of legitimacy within a given political community is often ongoing, even such contestation takes place in a context of intelligible disputes about what is contested. That is, not just anything will count as a serious criterion for political legitimacy in any particular context.
14. I have discussed Winch's views on political authority more fully in Horton (2005).
15. I am aware that I picked up the idea of using the Dalai Lama as an example to make this point from something I read. Unfortunately, I must apologize to its originator, as I cannot now remember where and have not been able to track down the source in order properly to acknowledge it.
16. For a helpful discussion of realism in political theory, see Galston (2010). My own reflections on the idea of a realist political theory can be found in Horton (2010b).

References

Beetham, D., 1991. *The legitimation of power*. Basingstoke: Macmillan.

Beran, H., 1987. *The consent theory of political obligation*. London: Croom Helm.

Bohman, J. and Richardson, H., 2009. Liberalism, deliberative democracy and 'reasons that all can accept'. *Journal of Political Philosophy*, 17 (3), 253–274.

Copp, D., 1999. The idea of a legitimate state. *Philosophy and Public Affairs*, 28, 3–45.

Freeman, S., 2007a. *Rawls*. London: Routledge.

Freeman, S., 2007b. *Justice and the social contract: essays on Rawlsian political philosophy*. Oxford: Oxford University Press.

Galston, W., 2010. Realism in political theory. *European Journal of Political Theory*, 9 (4), 385–411.

Horton, J., 2005. Peter Winch and political authority. *Philosophical Investigations*, 28 (3), 235–253.
Horton, J., 2010a. *Political obligation*. London: Palgrave Macmillan.
Horton, J., 2010b. Realism, liberal moralism and a political theory of modus vivendi. *European Journal of Political Theory*, 9 (4), 431–448.
Hume, D., 1987. Of the original contract. In: Essays: moral, political and legal. Indianapolis, IN: Liberty Classics.
Nagel, T., 1991. *Equality and partiality*. Oxford: Oxford University Press.
Nozick, R., 1974. *Anarchy, state and utopia*. Oxford: Basil Blackwell.
Rawls, J., 1999. *A theory of justice*. Oxford: Oxford University Press.
Schaar, J., 1969. Legitimacy and the modern state. *In*: P. Green and S. Levinson, eds. *Power and community*. New York, NY: Random House.
Simmons, A. J., 1979. *Moral principles and political obligations*. Princeton, NJ: Princeton University Press.
Simmons, A. J., 2001. *Justification and legitimacy: essays on rights and obligations*. Cambridge: Cambridge University Press.
Waldron, J., 1993. *Liberal rights: collected papers 1981–1991*. Cambridge: Cambridge University Press.
Williams, B., 2005. *In the beginning was the deed*. Princeton, NJ: Princeton University Press.
Winch, P., 1991. Certainty and authority. *In*: A. Phillips Griffiths, ed. *Wittgenstein centenary essays*. Cambridge: Cambridge University Press, 223–237.
Wolff, R. P., 1976. *In defense of anarchism*. New York, NY: Harper & Row.

Justice, legitimacy and (normative) authority for political realists

Enzo Rossi

Social Ethics Research Group, University of Wales, Newport, UK

One of the main challenges faced by realists in political philosophy is that of offering an account of authority that is genuinely normative and yet does not consist of a moralistic application of general, abstract ethical principles to the practice of politics. Political moralists typically start by devising a conception of justice based on their pre-political moral commitments; authority would then be legitimate only if political power is exercised in accordance with justice. As an alternative to that dominant approach I put forward the idea that upturning the relationship between justice and legitimacy affords a normative notion of authority that does not depend on a pre-political account of morality, and thus avoids some serious problems faced by mainstream theories of justice. I then argue that the appropriate purpose of justice is simply to specify the implementation of an independently grounded conception of legitimacy, which in turn rests on a context- and practice-sensitive understanding of the purpose of political power.

Introduction

Mainstream contemporary Anglo-American political philosophy tends to conceive of itself as a branch of applied ethics: the task of normative political theory would be that of guiding politics so as to promote or honour certain pre-political moral commitments. However, in recent years – under the labels of 'political realism'[1] or 'the realist critique of liberalism' – a radically different approach to political theory has begun to emerge and take the form of a recognizable if spontaneous current.[2] In a nutshell, realists contend that normative political theory should not try to silence, circumvent, contain or ignore the non-moral forces that shape politics – all tendencies that realists ascribe to mainstream contemporary political philosophy. In other words, political philosophy should not try to prescribe behaviour that runs against the grain of the practice of real politics.

A standard story in support of that approach has to do with the critique of purportedly 'purely normative' political theory as (an at least potential) expression of ideology. As Raymond Geuss puts it, 'ethics is usually dead politics: the hand of a victor in some past conflict reaching out to try to extend its grip to the present and the future' (Geuss 2008, p. 42) Another – related and vaguely Hobbesian – line of realist critique says that moralist political philosophy is ill-suited to its subject-matter: we need politics just because we disagree on ethics, so applied ethics-based political theory will not do (cf. Newey 2001, Williams 2005, Rossi 2010).[3]

One of the main aims of this paper is to advance the realist critique in a way that relies less on general observations of that sort – however convincing they may be – and more on a direct engagement with the object of its critique. I would like to show how adopting a realist approach can help us in making progress in debates where moralist theories are at an impasse.[4] More specifically, I will argue that debates on justice can be moved beyond a conflict between irreconcilable assumptions or intuitions if we abandon the moralist idea that justice is the first question of political philosophy.[5] Rather, legitimacy (as understood by realists) is the fundamental problem, and once a realist account of legitimacy is in place we will have a new angle from which to approach some seemingly intractable disagreements about justice.

That argument also takes on a wider challenge faced by realists in political philosophy, namely that of offering an account of authority that goes beyond the notion of *de facto* authority, i.e. an account that is genuinely normative and yet does not consist of a moralistic application of general, abstract ethical principles to the practice of politics. I would like to show that upturning the relationship between justice and legitimacy affords a normative notion of authority that does not depend on a pre-political account of morality. I argue that the appropriate purpose of justice is simply to specify the implementation of an independently grounded conception of legitimacy, which in turn rests on a context- and practice-sensitive understanding of the purpose of political power. Unlike mainstream approaches that take justice as their first question, by giving priority to (realist) legitimacy my proposed sequence makes it possible to specify the scope of application of our theory of justice in a freestanding way, allowing it to be genuinely normative and action guiding, but also grounded in an adequate account of the sphere it is meant to regulate.

The paper is structured as follows. The next section characterizes political moralism and argues that it fails to provide an adequate account of the scope of justice. The third section shows how that problem can be overcome through the priority of (realist) legitimacy over justice. The fourth and final section summarizes the argument and briefly canvasses some of the further questions it prompts.

Rejecting moralism

The view that justice is the fundamental subject-matter of political philosophy is closely connected to the moralistic approach to political philosophy, as I shall clarify shortly; so we begin with a thumbnail sketch of what I take to be the two ways in which mainstream political philosophy seeks to apply ethics to politics:[6]

- *Substantive/teleological approach:* the idea here is to set out an account of the good, and then devise the right (i.e. justice) accordingly. The paradigmatic example of this approach is utilitarianism, whereby justice requires the implementation of the set of rules that maximizes utility. The good is prior to the right on this approach, nonetheless the fundamental political–philosophical problems are still cashed out in terms of justice. The account of the good is presupposed and pre-political, so the role of political philosophy just is to work out a set of principles of right to maximize the good.
- *Procedural/deontological approach:* the aim here is to specify the right independently of the good.[7] Rawls's theory of justice is perhaps the most familiar example of this approach: some pre-political moral commitments are identified as constitutive of the concept of justice and are then formulated as a conception of justice through an appropriately specified procedure. Political–philosophical problems are then addressed by applying that conception.

As anticipated both approaches share the (moralistic) aspiration to guide political action on the basis of moral ideals (such as impartiality or well-being, say) that are external and prior to politics, in the sense that they are valued prior to and independently of any assessment of how suitable they are as organizing principles for the regulation of political matters in any particular context. In fact Geuss (2008, p. 9) calls this approach the 'ethics first' view, and Bernard Williams dubs it 'political moralism' (Williams 2005, p. 2). In a similar vein, Andrea Sangiovanni recently characterized the mainstream approach to justice as 'practice-independent':

> In each case, the principle of entitlement, utility, equality or priority (and the currency in which it is specified), is justified by appealing solely to moral values or to facts about human beings as such. No reference is made to existing institutions or practices, and the content, scope and justification of such principles in no way depend on the underlying structure of functioning of such practices and institutions. (Sangiovanni 2008, pp. 139–140)[8]

Now that characterization may well raise some important issues to do with the relation between moralism, fact-(in)sensitivity and ideal theory (Cohen 2003);[9] however, those issues are not of direct concern here. Rather, our focus should remain on the point that both variants of mainstream political philosophy try to achieve the priority of ethics over politics by affording centrality and priority to the question of justice. On the substantive approach justice is the means by which the moral ideal is implemented. On the procedural approach the role of justice is even more central: to implement the guiding moral ideal *just is* to implement a conception of justice.[10]

More precisely, my claim here is that moralism's reliance on pre-political moral commitments is a necessary and sufficient condition for the priority of justice. If we decide that the point of political philosophy is to specify how to implement some pre-political moral commitments, then we will think of our primary task as that of specifying a set of *rules* to bring about that implementation. Our conception of justice, then, is constituted by the specific rules we devise to implement our pre-political values.[11] Consistently with the distinction between the two variants of moralism outlined above, those rules and values may then be teleological or deontological, as the priority of justice is separate from the priority of the right over the good (Sandel 1998, pp. 2–3).[12] But the need to translate pre-political moral commitments into first-order principles of justice only explains why moralism is a sufficient condition for the priority of justice. The stronger claim that it is also a necessary condition can be explained by pointing out how, if we want justice to be 'the first virtue of social institutions' so that 'laws and institutions no matter how efficient and well-arranged must be reformed or abolished if they are unjust' (Rawls [1971] 1999, pp. 3), we need to draw on pre-political normative commitments exclusively: that categorical role can only be performed if justice is grounded in abstract moral ideals (or practice-independent in the sense seen above), lest our judgment be swayed by historically situated political contingencies such as a particular society's track record with the implementation of constitutional changes, say. In other words, if justice is to be the fundamental test for whether a political system stands or falls from the normative point of view, on pain of circularity the principles guiding judgments of justice should not be shaped by the nature of their subject-matter. However, as we will see in the next sub-section, this practice-independence spells serious difficulties for either version of the moralistic approach.

Given the relationship between moralism and the priority of justice, even if the two general arguments against moralism mentioned in the introductory section (the critical theory one and the Hobbesian one, neither of which I discuss here) were to fail, if the priority of justice can be shown to have undesirable effects moralism would still be undermined. But what could be wrong with the priority of justice? My contention is that moralist accounts of justice generate intractable controversies because they are incomplete. In a nutshell, my argument is this. The normative outcome of any theory of justice is partly determined by the scope of justice, but the scope of justice cannot be determined with reference to pre-political moral values. Since on the moralist approaches the salient content of any conception of justice is determined by pre-political values, those conceptions cannot contain an account of their scope. Therefore the moralist approaches yield incompleteness about matters of justice, in the sense that disagreements between competing moralist conceptions of justice cannot be adjudicated purely within the conceptual space of those theories. So, crudely, my claim is that moralist theories of justice talk past each other in a crucial respect.

Consider, for example, the familiar contrast in distributive justice theory between liberal egalitarians and libertarians on the issue of taxation and redistribution. The dispute is usually carried out in terms of the implications of self-ownership, or the nature of the basic structure, and so on. Typically the dialectic reaches an impasse where some basic intuitions conflict, as there is no widely shared adjudication methodology for such conflicts. My conjecture here is that the indeterminacy of those disagreements is due to a lack of agreement about the *scope* of justice. The scope question is the question of where coercive political power should reach. In other words, it is the question of which part of 'the political' should be regulated by the sort of norms laid out by political philosophy. If we begin from the scope question we will have a common ground on which to debate justice; but I want to argue that no moralist theory of justice can contain an account of its scope and, therefore, justice (as understood by moralists) cannot be the first question of political philosophy. Moralists want to start from a conception of justice, yet those conceptions are constituted by non-political ethical principles applied to politics, whereas determining the scope of justice is a question about the *nature of politics* itself. So we need to start from a realist theory of legitimacy instead, i.e. a theory of what politics is actually for in a given context.

For instance, in the case of the libertarian/egalitarian dispute, an account of the scope of justice would go a long way towards settling the issue of whether certain individual entitlements are defeasible (at least in a given context). Whether the state can legitimately redistribute a percentage of private income for particular purposes would no longer be a matter of whether such an exercise of political power is compatible with respect or promotion of certain abstract pre-political moral commitments (autonomy, rights, etc.); on a legitimacy driven realist approach the matter would be discussed as the partly empirical and hermeneutical issue of the meaning and purpose of politics in that particular context. And, as I will argue, that should provide a firmer basis for philosophical discussion than a clash of (allegedly) pre-political moral intuitions.

Before expounding the argument I just sketched it may be useful to lay out its bare structure:

> P1: An account of the scope of justice is necessary (but not sufficient) to determine the normative outcome of any theory of justice. So the scope is part of the normatively salient content of a theory of justice.
>
> P2: The normatively salient content of moralist conceptions of justice is entirely derived from pre-political moral values.

P3: An account of the scope of justice cannot be adequately provided with reference to pre-political moral values.

C1: Moralist conceptions of justice cannot adequately specify their scope. (From P1, P2, P3.)

C2: Moralist conceptions of justice are incomplete. (From P1, C1.)

First, what exactly is the scope of justice, and why does it matter to the normative outcome of a theory of justice? As we have seen, the scope of justice is the sphere that ought to be regulated by a theory of justice. Even if we simply maintained that the whole of 'the political' ought to be directly regulated by principles of justice we would need an account of why that should be the case. In Rawls's paradigmatic theory, the scope of justice is famously characterized through the idea of the basic structure of society (Rawls [1971] 1999, pp. 6–10, 1993, pp. 257ff.). Below I will argue that this characterization is unsatisfactory due to Rawls's moralism; but first we need to see how the account of the scope affects the normative content of a theory of justice. To continue with the example of justice as fairness, the point is simply that the parties in the original position know that they are selecting principles for the basic structure; so, for instance, the content of (say) the difference principle is shaped by both a normative commitment to impartiality and the need to shape 'the way in which the major social institutions distribute fundamental rights and duties and determine the division of advantage from social cooperation' (Rawls [1971] 1999, p. 7). More generally, principles of justice are always implicitly formulated on the basis of an account of their scope insofar as ought implies can, and to know what is possible we need to know what sphere a norm is supposed to regulate (among other things).

The second premise of my argument is the claim that the normatively salient content of moralist conceptions of justice is entirely derived from pre-political moral values. Here the thought is simply that most contemporary political philosophers' prescriptions are entirely derived from or at least justified in terms of the articulation of a set of politics-independent moral values – as shown in the account of the deontological and teleological approach above. In other words, if we think of the formulation of principles of justice as an input–processing–output operation, we may say that the input, or the raw material (as it were), is entirely constituted by those pre-political moral commitments. Again, consider Rawls's theory of justice as fairness (or at least its early formulation in the first edition of *A Theory of Justice*).[13] Moral intuitions on freedom, equality and impartiality are systematized through the method of reflective equilibrium, which in turn yields the normative commitments that inform the design of the original position. The resulting two principles of justice, then, are the result of a series of manipulations of those initial, pre-political moral commitments. The same is true of Robert Nozick's libertarianism, where entitlements are derived from an account of moral agency in a 'state of nature' (Nozick 1974, pp. 48ff.), or of various versions of consequentialism (which are rooted in a general moral account of well-being or perfection, say).

We can now move on to the third premise, namely why an adequate account of the scope of justice cannot be provided with reference to pre-political moral commitments (such as impartiality, reciprocity etc.), which are, however, the only source of the salient content of moralistic theories of justice. So the argument for this premise is in two steps: first I need to show that even the account of the scope in moralist theories of justice is derived from pre-political moral commitments, and then why that is not an adequate way of characterizing the scope of justice. The first step may appear particularly controversial. To take the example of justice as fairness again, one may just observe how Rawls has a separate account of the basic structure as the domain of application of his theory. But I wish to argue that Rawls's basic structure is not a satisfactory account of the scope of justice, because the pre-political normative commitments that give rise to the original position and the ensuing principles of justice also inform the account of the basic structure: 'once we think of the parties to a social contract as free and equal (and rational) moral persons, then there are strong reasons for taking the basic structure as the primary subject' (Rawls 1993, pp. 258–259). Put another way, even though the parties in the original position know that they have to work out principles of justice for the regulation of the basic structure, the account of the basic structure is informed by a prior understanding of what counts as background justice: 'We start with the basic structure and try to see how this structure itself should make the adjustments necessary to preserve background justice. [...] Certain background conditions are necessary if transactions between individuals are to be fair' (Rawls 1993, pp. 268–269).[14] That ethics-driven process is even more straightforward in the case of other moralistic theories of justice. As Rawls cogently argues, libertarian and utilitarian theories do not even have a special place for something akin to the basic structure, so they proceed directly from pre-political moral commitments to political prescriptions, making no principled distinctions between moral and political norms (pp. 262–265). Their account of the scope of justice, then, depends implicitly but entirely on their pre-political moral commitments: the account of the institutions to be regulated is just an implication of those commitments.

Now the second step of the argument for the third premise: what exactly is wrong with having an account of the scope of justice that depends on pre-political normative commitments? After all, while one may find fault with the way in which libertarianism and utilitarianism do not deal explicitly with the scope issue, Rawls's move may appear compelling, insofar as it explicitly specifies what institutions[15] we should regulate if we are committed to certain values.[16] But my contention is that that move begs the question of whether regulating those institutions rather than others is actually a pressing political problem, or simply becomes one if one has certain pre-political normative commitments. In other words, the problem is that moralist theories of justice do not really provide a freestanding account of their scope – they just spell out the implications of their pre-political normative commitments. And that is why they talk past each other: if the account of the scope is not grounded independently of the pre-political normative commitments, then we cannot have a debate on which principles are best suited to a given set of problems (despite the fact that debates are often framed in this way), and the substance of the disagreement is actually a clash between conflicting intuitions about the preferability of certain pre-political normative commitments over others.[17]

The three premises I just defended should lead us to the conclusion that moralist conceptions of justice do not have the resources to provide an adequate account of their own scope. They will of course presuppose such an account (for the reasons seen when discussing the first premise), but it will not be adequate in so far as it will be dependent on pre-political moral commitments.

If we accept the first conclusion we should also accept the second one: moralist conceptions of justice are incomplete, in the sense that their normative outcomes are not adequately determined (because their account of the scope of justice is not freestanding). This objection may arguably be presented as a kind of circularity charge: moralistic theories of justice present their normative outcome as a solution to the problems raised by the application of their pre-political normative commitments to an account of the scope of justice, but that account is itself dependent on those normative commitments. So the problem is characterized in a way that is biased towards the envisaged solution.[18] However, that may not be too serious a worry if there were no alternative way of formulating action-guiding principles for the exercise of political power; so in the reminder of this paper I shall attempt to show how a realist approach may overcome the difficulties I just pointed out.

The priority of legitimacy

To avoid the difficulty pointed out by my argument against the moralist priority of justice we need a freestanding account of the scope of justice, i.e. one that is not dependent on pre-political moral commitments. I argued that such an account cannot be provided within a theory of justice; in other words, the priority of justice is inescapably connected to moralism. That is why, as I will argue in this section, we need to move from moralism to realism, which involves taking legitimacy rather than justice as our first question.

Let me outline that move more thoroughly. Mainstream, moralist theories of justice begin from an account of what (pre-political) values should regulate the exercise of political power. They identify a set of relevant general moral commitments and proceed to apply them to politics, either in a substantive or in a procedural way. My argument in the previous section aimed to show that if the source material – as it were – of a normative political theory is entirely constituted by those pre-political moral commitments we cannot have an adequate account of the scope of justice. But of course we do need such an account, because any normative theory that aspires to be action-guiding needs an effective theory of justice. So the challenge is to devise an appropriate theorizing sequence that yields a theory of justice only after we have secured an independent account of the scope of justice. As anticipated, my suggestion is to start from a realist account of legitimacy, i.e. an empirically informed account of what politics is for in a given context. That, in turn, should allow us to adequately specify the scope of justice. The basic thought here is that, since the scope of justice is the sphere that ought to be regulated by principles of justice but cannot itself be adequately individuated through the pre-political moral commitments that constitute the salient content of moralistic accounts of justice, we need to recast the issue of scope as one to do mainly with the practice of politics itself, rather than the values that we would like to inform that practice. In other words, the question of where political power can legitimately reach should precede that of what principles should guide its exercise (call this the priority of legitimacy thesis), and it should be answered – at least in part – through an empirically informed account of the meaning and purpose of politics in the relevant cultural and historical context (call this the realist thesis).

To clarify that point it may be useful to explore the (somewhat stipulative)[19] distinction between the concepts of justice and legitimacy I am employing here. The question of *justice* is the question of what principles, rules, or *action-guiding norms* should regulate the exercise of political power in a given polity.[20] The question of *legitimacy*, on the other hand, concerns the *purpose* of the exercise of political power in a given polity. Crudely, justice tells us how to exercise political power, whereas legitimacy tells us what the exercise of political power is for – which should explain why I maintain that the latter should question be prior to the former. The two concepts are obviously related and it may even be possible to envisage conceptions of both that give them the same extension;[21] but my point here is simply to show how it is possible to drive a conceptual wedge between the norms that should regulate political action (justice) and the considerations that inform that choice of norms (legitimacy). In other words, legitimacy concerns the question of why we need politics in the first place, whereas justice concerns the rules through which politics should be regulated.

Now that characterization of the justice–legitimacy distinction should point us towards the way in which giving priority to a realist account of legitimacy can solve the problem with the scope of justice I described in the previous section. Recall how the moralistic priority of justice cannot yield a freestanding account of the scope of justice, i.e. of the limits of the sphere of action to be regulated by a conception of justice. In light of my argument we may say that, on the moralist approach, the difficulty with scope appears two pronged. On the one hand the priority of justice aspires to spell out action-guiding norms before specifying the purpose of those norms. On the other hand, drawing the account of the scope of justice from pre-political moral commitments fails to ensure that the scope encompasses genuine political concerns, rather than what counts as a political concern in light of certain pre-political moral commitments. So the two prongs are really the two sides of the same coin:[22] pre-political normative commitments cannot yield an adequate account of the scope of justice because they are geared towards generating general action-guiding principles, not an account of the purposes of politics in a given context. And it would not be possible to start from purpose-oriented pre-political commitments because we have seen (in 1.1 above) how moralism requires the priority of justice, and vice versa. That is why I maintain that the difficulty posed by the scope problem can only be overcome by starting our sequence of normative theorizing from a realist account of legitimacy: we need to start from an account of the deep purpose of the exercise of political power (i.e. of legitimacy), which justice (as defined above) cannot provide, and since that account cannot be grounded on pre-political moral commitments we need it to be empirically informed (i.e. realist).[23]

But how can we generate such an account of legitimacy, and does it yield genuinely normative and action-guiding notions of political authority and justice? In what follows I will sketch the general structure of a realist theory of legitimacy, and the way in which an adequate account of the scope of justice (and so an action-guiding conception of justice) can emerge from it.

One may ask in what sense, exactly, a realist account of legitimacy should be empirically informed, and what that implies with regard to the way in which the role of normative political theory is traditionally conceived. My suggestion would be to move beyond gesturing at a vaguely Weberian notion of legitimacy,[24] and answer both questions by drawing on Sangiovanni's (2008) account of practice-dependence in normative political theory. More specifically, while Sangiovanni puts forward a theory of practice-dependent *justice*, I would like to show how, in light of my argument against the priority of justice, the realist cause of practice-dependence is best served by a focus on *legitimacy.* That is not to say, of course, that there is no role for justice; my contention is simply that a realist and practice-dependent account of justice cannot stand alone or be our first question – it should rather descend from an account of legitimacy.

Sangiovanni's practice-dependent account of justice explicitly incorporates many insights from the realist critique of mainstream political philosophy.[25] Most importantly for our present purposes, it offers a hermeneutic approach to the articulation of the empirical component of any realist approach to normative political theory:

> The content, scope, and justification of a conception of justice depends on the structure and form of the *practices* that the conception is intended to govern. [Therefore] in justifying any conception of justice, we first need an *interpretation* both of the point and *purpose* of the institutions that the conception is intended to govern, and of the role principles are intended to play within them. (Sangiovanni 2008, pp. 138, 141; added emphasis)

I will not rehearse Sangiovanni's argument for practice-dependence,[26] as my argument from the scope of justice should already have established the case for realism. What I do wish to establish now, however, is that the argument from the scope of justice should also lead us to a form of realism that proceeds from a practice-dependent account of justice to an action-guiding account of justice, rather than yielding a freestanding conception of justice. Simplifying somewhat, Sangiovanni maintains that the existence of institutional systems gives rise to peculiar relations between persons, and those relations in turn generate a demand for regulation through a conception of justice. The way to devise such a conception, then, is to interpret the purpose of those institutions in a way that is sufficiently critically aware to generate a normative assessment of existing arrangements as well as action-guiding principles of justice. But Sangiovanni recognizes a potential difficulty with that move:

> We may be worried that in interpreting an institutional system in this way, we must apply standards of value that we already endorse independently of the institutions we are considering. Without such initial assessment of value, we will not be able to make sense of the point and purpose of a practice or activity. [...] And this may seem to make the interpretive step in the justification of a conception of justice viciously circular. (Sangiovanni 2008, p. 149)

To address that worry Sangiovanni points out that the interpretation of existing practices is only an initial and provisional step. The conception of justice cannot be entirely derived from the interpretive understanding of institutions; that understanding must be 'extended' into a further, critical stage. While 'without the constraints provided by the interpretive step, justice [...] would have neither a determinate content nor an application', taking those constraints into account is not sufficient to derive a conception of justice. To complete the critical stage, then, we need to 'move from the point and purpose of institutions and the reasons those involved have for affirming them, to the way they shape relations among participants' (Sangiovanni 2008, p. 150). Presumably those relations are to be critically assessed by the lights of freestanding, perhaps even pre-political normative commitments that are able to yield action-guiding principles.[27]

Therefore, it would appear that, by delaying the introduction of those normative commitments until after the interpretation of the point and purpose of the relevant institutions, Sangiovanni has managed to avoid the moralistic pitfall of characterizing the scope of justice through the distorting lens of abstract, pre-political moral values. However, if we pay closer attention to the interpretive stage we should come to realize that, while Sangiovanni may well have dispelled the circularity worry in the terms in which he formulated it, my account of the problem of the scope of justice could be recast it in a more insidious way. The problem is that Sangiovanni's interpretive process is geared towards picking out the features of institutions that are relevant to some prior notion of justice: 'the aim of the interpretive stage is to establish the parameters and fixed points which a full-blown conception of justice must take into account. [It] is meant to provide structure to the justification of a conception of justice' (Sangiovanni 2008, p. 149). Interpreting a practice through the lens of a concept of justice cannot yield a freestanding account of the scope of justice, i.e. the sphere of action that ought to be regulated by normative political theory. In other words, how do we know (without projecting our own pre-political normative commitments, that is) whether a certain practice is meant to contribute to the establishment of justice? It seems to me that, in looking for justice at the interpretive stage, Sangiovanni skipped a step of the sequence required by a genuinely realistic mode of normative theorizing. As anticipated, my suggestion would be to postpone the search for justice until we have an account of legitimacy; so, if the interpretive stage is to genuinely explore the 'point and purpose' of institutions, it should rather focus on drawing out an account of legitimacy.[28] That is because, unlike justice, legitimacy is actually about the purpose of the exercise of political power,[29] so using it as a hermeneutic lens will not cause any distortion, as it were. Such a genuinely freestanding account of the purposes of politics in a given context will then yield an adequate account of the scope of justice, and on that basis, as envisaged in Sangiovanni's critical stage of realist theorizing, we will of course be able to devise suitably action-guiding principles of justice.

Conclusion

Let us now briefly review the paper's argument. I started by identifying a tendency, in mainstream contemporary political philosophy, to generate action-guiding principles whose salient content is drawn entirely from pre-political moral commitments. This moralistic tendency is strictly tied to the idea that justice is the first question of political philosophy. I then argued that, however, the moralistic approach yields inadequate theories of justice, insofar as it is unable to provide a freestanding account of the scope of justice, i.e. of the boundaries of the sphere of the exercise of political power that ought to be regulated by principles of justice. To overcome that difficulty I proposed to give priority to the question of legitimacy over justice, understanding the former in an empirically informed, realist way. I then showed how a realist account of legitimacy can generate a practice-dependent but genuinely normative conception of justice. In that way the realist approach to political philosophy can move beyond the notion of mere de facto authority and carve some space for a critical and action-guiding alternative to mainstream political moralism.

To be sure, my argument points to a number of open questions. Tackling them in any detail, or even listing them, would be beyond the scope of this paper; yet, in order to sketch a possible direction for the realist research programme, it may be helpful to mention what may well be the most pressing worry, namely whether practice-dependence does not place excessive constraints upon the sort of prescriptions that a theory may envisage – however, the realist may well point out that a solid grounding in a context's factual constraints is the best platform on which to construct radical alternatives (Geuss 2010, pp. x–xi). The challenge, then, becomes that of tackling the descriptive and hermeneutic element of political theory in a way that is sufficiently critically aware to pave the way for realistic normative solutions.

Acknowledgments

Various versions of this paper were presented at the Central European University, Bayreuth University, the University of Wales – Newport, and Warwick University. I am grateful to all audiences for their feedback. I would also like to thank Emanuela Ceva, Chandran Kukathas, Richard North and Janosch Prinz for their helpful written comments.

Notes

1. Not to be confused, of course, with the related but much more circumscribed realist tradition in international relations theory.
2. The work of theorists as disparate as William Connolly, John Dunn, John Gray, Bonnie Honig, John Horton, Chantal Mouffe, Glen Newey, Mark Philp, Judith Shklar and Bernard Williams is beginning to be seen as contributing to the development of a the realist literature. For an overview, see Sangiovanni (2009) and Galston (2010).
3. Rawlsians might object that the project of political liberalism is precisely that of overcoming disagreements about comprehensive conceptions of the good by relying on political ideas of the good. That response elicits at least two separate rejoinders. On the one hand, some realists (Sangiovanni 2008, Sleat 2010) have put forward an interpretation of Rawls's later work that highlights

its more context- and practice-sensitive aspects; but it also seems fair to say that much of mainstream political philosophy has not followed in the footsteps of what some have seen as Rawls's departure from moralism (in fact that aspect has attracted much criticism from Rawls's own followers (cf., for example, Scheffler 1994). On the other hand, the political–comprehensive distinction has been subjected to a number of powerful criticisms (e.g. Gaus 1999), so simply pointing to it will not be enough to fend off the realist challenges.

4. This paper's main focus is simply the realist critique of mainstream political philosophy, rather than the formulation of an alternative first-order realist theory of justice. For a sense of what the latter might look like, Sangiovanni (2008) provides examples of how a broadly realist approach can help us making progress on a number of familiar questions such as the right to free speech and the justification of human rights in a global context.
5. The *incipit* of Rawls's *A Theory of Justice* ([1971] 1999) comes to mind here. I will return to it below.
6. Williams (2005, p. 3) puts forward a similar distinction between the 'enactment' and the 'structural' model of political philosophy.
7. Set aside the familiar question – which I have discussed in Rossi (2009) – of whether procedural accounts of justice need to rely on a substantive account of desirable outcomes. On this issue, see also Ceva (2009, 2012) and Newey (2012).
8. One may object that Rawls's notion of a realistic utopia is meant to anticipate precisely this sort of charge. Yet, arguably, Sangiovanni's notion of practice-dependence (to which I will return below) is more context specific and thus more demanding than Rawls's rather abstract concern with laws of nature, 'persons' moral and psychological natures' and 'general facts about human society' (Rawls 1999, pp. 119, 175).
9. For a critical discussion, see Guay (2009).
10. This discussion provisionally presupposes the viability of Rawls's distinction between the concept and the conceptions of justice.
11. I will spell out this point in more detail in my discussion of the justice–legitimacy distinction in the third section below.
12. Not only Kant, but also J. S. Mill give priority to justice, at least at the first-order level (but, unlike Kant, not at the level of justification).
13. Since the 1980s Rawls has progressively been introducing contextual elements in his account of justice (on this point, see Sangiovanni 2008), so his position has become increasingly less moralistic. However, for present purposes, it will be necessary to focus on clear-cut cases of moralist approaches to justice.
14. Set aside, for now, the issue of whether this need for a prior understanding of the notion of background justice makes the original position a somewhat circular decision procedure.
15. I use the word 'institutions' in a deliberately loose and wide-ranging way here. One may however note that, as Christopher Bertram has persuasively argued (Bertram 2010), much of the literature on the basic structure tends to blur two conceptions of that concept: a quasi-legal one, focused on rules and institutions, and a sociological one, focused on broader features of society. My argument should be able to range over that distinction.
16. However, if my analysis is correct, at a deeper level the account of the basic structure does not mark a significant structural difference between justice as fairness and libertarianism or utilitarianism.
17. Here one might object that *some* normative assumptions are needed to begin to identify the normatively salient features of a political context, and so the moral-

istic way of construing the scope of justice is inevitable. I do not deny that my reply would be simply to point out that, on the moralist approach, *all* of the salient content of the scope is derived from pre-political moral commitments.

18. I will not discuss whether my argument should be considered fatal to the moralist approach to justice, as that judgment is best left to the reader; but I do hope to have at least shown that incompleteness is a serious shortcoming.
19. While a degree of stipulation is inevitable when dealing with contestable concepts such as justice and legitimacy, that should not pose serious problems here, insofar as my argument simply aims to show a sequence of steps that lead to adequately grounded action-guiding principles. What names we attach to those steps is not crucial.
20. Set aside the familiar questions of whether all political power is exercised by the state, or whether justice need only concern the political power exercised by the state, and so on (cf. Cohen 2011, p. 227) – my argument is general enough to range over the various possible answers to those questions.
21. If, for instance, we maintained that a state is legitimate if and only if it is just.
22. That is unsurprising, as we saw that the relationship between the priority of justice and moralism is a bi-conditional.
23. In discussing the need for the empirical grounding of a realist conception of legitimacy both Williams (2005, p. 9) and Geuss (2008, pp. 34–36) refer to the exemplar of Weber's seminal work, which, regrettably, has been largely neglected by post-Rawlsian political philosophy. Relatedly, until the last few years David Beetham has been a relatively lone voice in putting forward the view that the normative and descriptive aspects of legitimacy cannot be disentangled (Beetham 1991). I will return to this general issue below.
24. See note 23.
25. In fact, Sangiovanni (2008, 158n, 163n) points out the close connections between his views and those of Williams, Geuss, and even Weber and Morgenthau.
26. Nor, more specifically, his argument for the particular form of practice-dependence he favours, namely one focused on institutional rather than cultural practices.
27. Sangiovanni (2008, pp. 150–156) clarifies this point through an interpretation of Rawls's theory of justice as fairness in its later recasting as well as through a discussion of a number of aspects of recent debates on global justice. I take those illustrations to be successful, so I will not provide examples here.
28. Therefore, we may say that Sangiovanni's practice-dependence yields a *contextualist* position about justice. But I maintain that contextualism is not enough of a departure from moralism to overcome the problem of the scope of justice; for that we need the priority of legitimacy, which yields a full-blown *realist* position (as contextualism is just a component of realism).
29. See the third section.

References

Beetham, D., 1991. *The legitimation of power*. Basingstoke: Palgrave Macmillan.
Bertram, C., 2010. Institutions and the limits of procedural justice. Unpublished manuscript. Bristol: Department of Philosophy, University of Bristol.
Ceva, E., 2009. Just procedures with controversial outcomes: on the grounds for substantive disputation within a procedural theory of justice. *Res Publica*, 15 (3), 219–235.
Ceva, E., 2012. Beyond legitimacy: can proceduralism say anything relevant about justice? *Critical Reviews of International Social and Political Philosophy* (this issue).
Cohen, G. A., 2003. Facts and principles. *Philosophy and Public Affairs*, 31 (3), 211–245.
Cohen, G. A., 2011. How to do political philosophy. *In*: *On the currency of egalitarian justice and other essays in political philosophy*. Princeton, NJ: Princeton University Press, 225–235.
Galston, W. A., 2010. Realism in political theory. *European Journal of Political Theory*, 9 (4), 385–411.
Gaus, G. F., 1999. Reasonable pluralism and the domain of the political: how the weaknesses of John Rawls's political liberalism can be overcome by a justificatory liberalism. *Inquiry* 42 (2), 259–284.
Geuss, R., 2008. *Philosophy and Real Politics*. Princeton, NJ: Princeton University Press.
Geuss, R., 2010. *Politics and the Imagination*. Princeton, NJ: Princeton University Press.
Guay, R., 2009. On being constrained by the facts: Cohen on facts and principles. Unpublished manuscript, Department of Philosophy, SUNY Binghampton, NY.
Newey, G., 2001. *After politics*. London: Palgrave Macmillan.
Newey, G., 2012. Just politics. *Critical Reviews of International Social and Political Philosophy* (this issue).
Nozick, R., 1974. *Anarchy, state and utopia*. New York: Basic Books.
Rawl, J., 1993. *Political liberalism*. New York: Columbia University Press.
Rawls, J., [1971] 1999. *A theory of justice*. Cambridge, MA: Belknap.
Rawls, J., 1999. *The law of peoples: with 'the idea of public reason revisited'*. Cambridge, MA: Harvard University Press.
Rossi, E., 2009. The exemption that confirms the rule: reflections on proceduralism and the UK hybrid embryos controversy. *Res Publica* 15 (3), 237–250.
Rossi, E., 2010. Reality and imagination in political theory and practice. on Raymond Geuss' realism. *European Journal of Political Theory*, 9 (4), 204–212.
Sandel, M., 1998. *Liberalism and the limits of justice*. 2nd edition. Cambridge: Cambridge University Press.
Sangiovanni, A., 2008. Justice and the priority of politics to morality. *Journal of Political Philosophy*, 16 (2), 137–164.
Sangiovanni, A., 2009. Normative political theory: a flight from reality? *In*: D. Bell, ed. *Political thought and international relations*. Oxford: Oxford University Press, 219–239.
Scheffler, S., 1994. The appeal of political liberalism. *Ethics* 105 (1), 4–22.
Sleat, M., 2010. Bernard Williams and the possibility of a realist political theory. *European Journal of Political Theory*, 9 (4), 485–503.
Williams, B., 2005. Realism and moralism in political theory. *In*: *In the beginning was the deed*. Princeton, NJ: Princeton University Press, 1–17.

Just politics

Glen Newey

Université Libre de Bruxelles, Brussels, Belgium

This paper asks whether political justice can be encapsulated by procedures. It examines John Rawls's tripartite distinction between perfect, pure and imperfect procedural justice, concluding that none gives a satisfactory account of procedural justice. Imperfect procedural justice assumes that there could be an authoritative source of justice other than procedures, while perfect procedural justice takes a double-minded view of procedure-independent standards of justice. That leaves pure procedural justice as an apparently decisionistic mode of deciding which outcomes are just. This at least avoids the confusion between having authoritative procedures and procedure-independent standards that are also purportedly authoritative. However, it is argued that even a political procedure that defines the extension of a term such a 'justice' will lack authority over it once its reference is fixed. Since Rawls's categories of procedural justice are jointly exhaustive, the problem of determining justice via political procedures appears insoluble.

Introduction

How far can politics[1] respond to the demands of justice? Of course, this is an ancient question, posed in antiquity by Plato and others. It is unclear how far Plato himself gives it an affirmative answer. While the *Republic* and *Laws* certainly call for government, their regimes merely implement agreed norms via established procedures, and this does not get as far as politics. For one thing, the very *possibility* of conflict seems to be ruled out in advance, and this is inimical to politics. Second, how the principles are generated threatens to subvert their authority. In Plato's dialogues, their authority relies squarely on the force of the stronger argument. Third, there is little sense that politics is a sometimes *ad hoc* response to events beyond bureaucratic control.

But the Platonic construction seems better motivated within a concern for justice. Given that concern, it is natural, even compelling, to think that justice must be effected via a set of principles. However, if the project involves implementing principles rather than debating them, or dealing with conflicts between them and other desiderata, the focus shifts away from politics, to what Engels, following Saint-Simon, called 'the administration of things' – a claim advanced in a work that aims to *distance* Marxian socialism from its 'utopian' rival (Engels 1975, p. 41).[2] This is also plainly the case with liberal theories of distributive justice, as in Rawlsian theory. Maintaining distributive shares demands agreement on the principles, and their priority over other political goals.

This prompts the question whether the tension between politics and bureaucratized principles of justice is avoidable.[3] Can there be a politics of justice, or is there just politics?

Job

In the Bible story, Job suffers a series of personal disasters, including the death of his children, the destruction of his house and disfiguring disease. He complains that God has treated him unjustly (Job XXXI). God makes no attempt to justify what has happened to Job by referring it to some scheme of cosmic justice. Instead God simply reasserts the brute fact of His overwhelming might. He specifically repudiates the claims of Job's erstwhile friends (his 'comforters') who try to vindicate God's treatment of him via independent claims of justice. Job's rehabilitation follows when he stops questioning the Almighty and submits himself to divine power.

One might think that Job's story lies so firmly within an order of traditional beliefs that it has little to say to modern democratic societies. I shall however argue that our predicament in the face of political power is closer to Job's than liberals may find comfortable. The argument focuses on the generic conditions of politics itself. Though politics is simply given, as a condition of collective life, little content in politics is given, apart from the use of power. In proceduralism the use of power is legitimated by procedures whose *outcomes* lack non-procedural justification; that turns attention to the justification of the procedures, which are enforced by the use of power. Democratic politics invite us as citizens to see ourselves in the position both of God and of Job, as wielders and subjects of power. As subjects citizens want limits on this power. But as wielders of it, they face the 'teleological suspension of the ethical' (Kierkegaard 1985, p. 59) – they cannot use the ethical itself to decide whether the ethical itself should dictate to power.

I argue below that politics cannot be coherently fitted to a prefabricated moral or ethical ideal, via a critique of Rawls's distinction between perfect, imperfect and procedural justice. The main question I ask is: Can the justice of political outcomes be specified independently of the procedures that yield them? I cast doubt on whether this is possible. The issue is the *authority* enjoyed by a presented set of principles of justice, particularly in relation to the accompanying procedures. If political justification is closed under justifiable procedure, then the authority of their outcomes, such as principles of justice, depends on their having been generated by the procedures. But then the idea of an independent standard of justice proves chimerical.[4]

While the prospects for any ground-up approach to political design may be bleak, my argument does not imply, with some of the blanker versions of realism, that there is nothing to politics beyond power-play. One reason for this is that political institutions and procedures, which form part of the raw material of politics, are in part the precipitates of ethical ideas. Another, Weberian, reason is that legitimating discourse puts real limits on what political actors can think and do (Skinner 2002, esp. ch. 4).

Procedural justice and the authority question

The classic discussion of procedural justice appears in John Rawls's *A Theory of Justice* (1971, pp. 83ff.). I will use his tripartite distinction between *pure, perfect* and *imperfect* procedural justice to frame my own discussion. Rawls does not present the distinction in an analytically systematic way. But it seems that he conceives of the three kinds of procedural justice as mutually exclusive and jointly exhaustive. If that is right, the prospects for procedural justice stand or fall with the viability of these alternatives: that is, only if one of the three is a workable conception of justice is there a workable form of procedural justice.

Imperfect procedural justice

For Rawls, political procedures at best embody *imperfect procedural justice.* That is, even justifiable political procedures will foreseeably give rise to outcomes which are substantively not just, or perhaps even unjust, as judged by the theory that first generated the procedures. So presumably the failings of public policy which prompted liberal theorists to devise theories of civil disobedience (e.g. Bedau 1991) or of conscientious refusal,[5] will arise not only with societies which are not well-ordered and so are deemed to require a theory of 'partial compliance' (Rawls 1971, pp. 245–248), but also with those societies which, though well-ordered, generate non-just outcomes because political procedures cannot but be imperfectly just. There is, then, a question about the justificatory relation between the procedures which theory justifies, and the non-ideal outcomes that the procedures may throw up.

Someone may object that if the procedures themselves are designed either to stipulate or to reflect what is just, then they cannot go wrong in the way Rawls suggests. Suppose, for instance, that it is said that a set of political procedures is justified if and only if nobody could reasonably reject it (Scanlon 1998, Barry 1955). If it is to have any content, the corresponding account of political design[6] will presumably specify a set of procedures to meet this justificatory demand, e.g. ones that give each person an equal say in determining political outcomes. Then, since justifiable procedures in turn justify the outcomes they yield, no procedure that gives each person an equal say could yield an outcome that anyone could reasonably reject. If giving everyone an equal say guarantees the justifiability of the outcome – to create an outcome that nobody could reasonably reject – justifiability will be closed under the correct application of a valid procedure, just as truth is closed under valid inference.

However, one can deny that the justification of procedures must coincide with an account of how the political outcomes they yield can be justified. This is inherent in the notion of imperfect procedural justice. If one assumes there is an independent standard that ratifies the outcomes, then procedures that the theory treats as justified may sometimes yield unjustifiable outcomes. Rawls seems to put this down to the fact that the procedures do not embody *perfect* procedural justice: procedures that guarantee the justice of their outcome, if followed correctly (Rawls 1971, pp. 84–85). That is because he believes that there is an independent standard to gauge the justice of outcomes, at least in principle. The explicit paradigm is forensic procedure as a method for determining criminal guilt. Rawls takes it that even conscientiously administered procedures will sometimes err in their judgments of fact. The question, however, is how judgments outside the system for deciding outcomes can claim *authority* – and specifically, the authority to trump supposed authoritative procedures.

Perfect procedural justice

But need the procedures be flawed? Consider Rawls's second possibility, namely perfect procedural justice, whereby the procedures always deliver outcomes that meet an independent standard of justice. There is a genuinely independent standard of justice, and happily the procedure has been so designed that its outputs always meet it. But does 'perfect procedural justice' really name a third way between 'pure' and 'imperfect' procedural justice? The question arises when one asks what guarantees that the standard of justice really is independent of the procedure that creates the outcomes. Take Rawls's own example of cutting a cake (Rawls 1971, p. 85): carrying out the operation according to the rule *Whoever who cuts the cake takes the last slice* will guarantee equal division: assuming that the cutter wants to have as much cake as possible, judges that the others are similarly motivated for themselves and acts rationally. These are empirical and contingent assumptions, but the hypothesis of limited altruism and scarcity are presumably needed to make the circumstances those of justice to start with.

However, if *equality* is thought of as the independent standard of justice, it can still be debated whether an equal division is justified, all things considered. It is assumed that the independent standard calls for equal shares.

But maybe contextual notions of need, desert or voluntary exchange will disrupt equality.[7] Perhaps the thing to go for is equal shares. But this will necessarily not be guaranteed by methods of perfect, as opposed to pure, procedural justice, if standard and procedure really are independent. If the procedure *does* guarantee equality, we have relapsed into pure procedural justice. The procedure is adopted so as to get equal shares, and the results of applying it are not independent of the basis for choosing it. The protocol *Whoever cuts the cake takes the last slice* is likely to be chosen, with the background assumptions, only if those choosing it already wish to ensure equality.

We can see this from a different angle by asking about the *conditions* in which conceptions of justice are enforced. In Rawls's example, equality, interpreted as requiring that each person gets a same-sized share of the cake, has already been chosen.[8] Given this, the protocol will yield the desired outcome, given the assumptions in play, as it has been chosen so as to produce equality. Procedures are, indeed, sometimes chosen to yield a target outcome, as in using a gauge to screen out oversized baggage at airport departure gates. Such a procedure is like a valve that lets through only those outcomes that fit a specification. Since the procedure has been selected to achieve the goal, it is not independent of that goal. Had some other outcome been sought, such as permitting shares to vary only within prescribed bounds, or screening out only baggage over a certain *weight*, another procedure would have been adopted. It remains to be shown, then, that a standard of justice can be both independent of procedure and infallibly duplicate its outcomes.

If the standard can show that the outcome of the procedures may be defective even when the procedures have been correctly followed, it must be independent of the procedures themselves.[9] The procedure may go wrong, as judged by an independent standard of justice, when it is applied to specific decisions about who gets what. If it really is independent, the standard will leave open the possibility, *ex ante*, that the outcomes may not be justified after all, despite having been generated by the procedures. Of course it is possible to insure against this by selecting a procedure, as in the cake-cutting case, that guarantees the outcome dictated by a standard such as equality. But then neither outcome nor procedure is independent of that standard. The notion of 'perfect' procedural justice, distinct from its 'pure' counterpart, proves chimerical.

Even in the simple cake-cutting case, the decision about which standard to go for will rest on various circumstantial factors. The standard itself cannot determine fully the conditions in which it is applied: that depends on operational decisions. Even if it could, it would still not be independent of the procedure. Sometimes, of course, the outcomes will go awry, as judged by free-standing criteria of justice, because the procedures themselves have been maladministered. A suitably flexible set of procedures may incorporate homeostatic mechanisms such as judicial review. But these mechanisms are prey to the same defects as the original procedures. For instance, judicial review may reverse an initially justified outcome, or ratify an unjustified one. Even sophisticated procedures will realize only imperfect procedural justice. If there is a genuinely independent standard of justice, there is always the possibility that even scrupulously followed procedures will throw up outcomes at variance with it.

It might be objected that if the procedures are zealously applied and duly accoutred with the self-correcting mechanisms, they could conform reliably to an independent standard of justice. Did Rawls nod in cleaving to the belief, which gets little direct argumentative support in *Theory of Justice*, that the procedures of even well-ordered societies would be only imperfectly just?[10] Is there some deep fact about either the world or attempts to regiment it procedurally, which dooms them to imperfection? I assume that it is uncontroversial that procedures cannot be infallibly administered, so the outcomes they generate can go wrong simply for that reason. What is harder to accept, however, is that the justified procedures can be so finessed that this is the only infirmity from which they can suffer. No procedure, even one impeccably applied, can guarantee outcomes that are substantively just. There is always the possibility of disequilibrium, not only in the process of constructing the theory itself, but in the outcomes of its favoured procedures, given an authoritative basis for judging that the outcomes have gone awry.[11]

There are several reasons why this is so, some of which Rawls himself recognized in *Political Liberalism* (1996). Procedures subsume particulars under a nomic concept, such as that of justice. The broader the concept, the greater the scope for uncertainty as to whether or not a given particular, such as a proposed course of action, falls under it. Formal systems are procedures for deriving outcomes via rules of validity, just as rules of inference aim to derive theorems via stereotyped forms of action in accord with rules. Properly applied, the procedures may lead to outcomes which are substantively unjust, when judged by the understanding of justice which gave rise to the procedures. Nothing guarantees that the procedures will not yield outcomes which are, judged by the rationale for the procedures themselves, anomalous; at least, given an authoritative standard relative to which the notion of *anomaly* applies. Since standards can vary from the outcomes of procedures, however designed, there is the question whether the outcome or the standard – embodied, say, in the individual conscience – should be treated as authoritative. As with its imperfect counterpart, perfect procedural justice comes to grief on the issue of authority.

Pure procedural justice

Pure procedural justice makes the procedures themselves the means by which the justice of their outcome is decided. If they embody pure procedural justice, the procedures result in a form of political decisionism. The fact that they arose from the procedures is what makes the outcomes right, just as truth is preserved under valid entailment. Suppose that there are various evaluative dimensions relevant to determining the justice of some outcome, as viewed independently of the procedures which yielded it. There is no standpoint from which the judgment that, say, the outcome is unjust can be *authoritatively* asserted, though the doctrine of reasonable pluralism allows, of course, that individuals may reasonably assert or deny that judgment. The doctrine of the burdens of judgment, which underlies Rawls's case for reasonable pluralism in *Political Liberalism* and elsewhere, holds that variations in experiences, the complexity of concepts, different weighting of factors relevant to judgment, the ambiguity of evidence, and plural values mean that reasonable people, left free to decide for themselves, will arrive at different ideas of the good life.

The burdens may well be set features of our epistemic predicament. But, insofar as they are, they preclude designing procedures that satisfactorily embody a complex concept such as that of justice. This is true not only because the procedures build in intuitions about justice, but also because they predictably create the outcomes that answer to these ideas. Once again, the spectre of disequilibrium looms, in the foreseeable mismatch between actual outcomes and intuitive ideas of justice. The burdens of judgment foretell this mismatch. They predict that the outcomes may be judged unjust on the strength of people's experiences, idiosyncratic weighting of evidence, and so on. Hence the theory itself can be taken to predict that its favoured procedures are imperfectly just, to the extent that their outcomes are reasonably rejectable.

However, one may respond that the burdens show only that some people will *judge* that a given procedurally created outcome is unjust. One can ask how much authority such a judgment commands. But this does not really dispose of the problem. For one thing, people who freely arrive at the judgment that an outcome is unjust presumably count as reasonable, since it is accepted that reasonable people reach judgments despite the burdens.[12] More importantly, an objector who urges that the judgment lacks authority will do so from within a commitment to the bindingness of the procedures, e.g. because the procedures are seen as just. Someone who thought with Rawls that the burdens were important in justifying the procedures would also be likely to think that they should come into play when assessing the procedures' upshot. Further, if moral ideals of justice really have the authority to justify and shape political procedures, we need to know why these same ideals lack the authority to correct the procedures' results if they go wrong. If they do not lack it, the possibility of conscientious refusal, and so on, must be endemic not only in partially just, but also in well-ordered societies.[13]

However, Rawls's later espousal of reasonable pluralism tends to erode the extra-procedural basis for authoritative judgments. Applying the burdens to a disputed outcome means that it may be indeterminate whether or not the upshot of the procedures really is just, when measured by some independent standard.[14] The same goes for any consideration other than justice on which one might judge whether or not an outcome is acceptable. The political construction has to be insulated against reasonable pluralism. It is not that the judgments that query a procedural outcome may not be correct; it is that something has to give these judgments political authority. One could ask why the scope of the burdens should be limited to these judgments, and not applied also to the macro-level judgments, for example about justice, which the theory itself makes, and enter into the content of the public conception of justice. That looks like an arbitrary stipulation. But if the burdens can bear on the political construction itself, the game is up.

Assuming, however, that this problem is dealt with, as it must be if Rawls's political construction is to work, the well-ordered society will display pure procedural justice. Decisionism then surfaces in the impossibility of asserting an authoritative judgment within a commitment to proceduralism and reasonable pluralism. The later Rawls thus emerges, somewhat surprisingly, as being at least in this respect a prophet of realism. Of course, the doctrine of an independent moral standard acting as a check on political outcomes can still be found in the work of political moralists. It appears, for example in Dworkin's work, as the survival of charismatic authority, embodied in the moral judgments of the judiciary (Dworkin 1986). But even here, procedures vest some individuals' judgments with decisive authority.

Procedures and justice

One could argue that procedures need not instantiate an ideal of justice at all.[15] It has been argued that it is far easier to identify *gross* injustice, such as slavery, than ideal justice. This would be a more minimal idea of the just (or not-unjust) state. Procedural outcomes would be legitimate insofar as they avoided gross injustice. Space prevents discussing this idea at length. I will make the following brief comments. First, its appeal may stem not from the intuitive primacy of injustice over justice, but of examples over their generalization: there are intuitively compelling cases of justice, too, such as giving identically situated individuals identical shares. Examples allow indefinitely many projections into general principles. Even the notion of a *gross injustice* leaves room for disagreement, particularly when translated into principles and thence into procedures. Second, the gross injustice idea admits the same treatment as the ideal–theoretic approach. One can institutionalize ways of avoiding gross injustice, to which the Rawlsian taxonomy can apply: for instance, by making respect for persons a side-constraint on outcomes, as in human rights law, which minimally precludes gross violations of respect such as torture. To that extent, the foregoing remarks apply to gross injustice: actual procedures cannot guarantee capturing the ideal of *in*justice adequately. Insofar as negative ideals have less content than positive ones, though, gaps between procedural and ideal may open up less obviously and less often.

But in any case the suggestion that gross injustice is theoretically less problematic than justice does not really dispose of the problem facing perfect procedural justice, which stems from equivocation over whether standards of justice are really independent of procedures. That remains true even if we can more confidently articulate an ideal of gross injustice than one of justice. Perfect procedural justice rests on the idea that outcomes may vary independently of an external standard, while infallibly echoing that standard because they flow from procedures chosen to yield precisely those outcomes that meet it. So, perfect procedural justice still appears chimerical even in the case of gross injustice.

What does this leave? I have already suggested that reasonable disagreement (Rawls 1996, pp. 54–66)[16] calls in question whether imperfect procedural justice is coherent. Imperfect procedural justice sets a standard of justice that real-world procedures aim to track. But they will do so only fallibly. An external norm is supposed to gauge the justice of real outcomes. It is accepted that outcomes delivered by real procedures may fall short. But then what is the 'external' standard of justice that is brought to bear in the case of imperfect procedural justice? There is no obvious method, analogous to radio-carbon dating, that can give an objective reading to back up other archaeological data. Radiometric dating embodies an objective standard against which to judge interpretations of these data. But with justice, no such standard lies to hand. Even if there are objective truths about justice, they do not exist in a form which can be used in assessing the justice of actions – one of the disquieting aspects of the Job story.

On the basis of the burdens, a citizen who disputed a given political outcome (for example, because he thought it was unjust) would have no warrant for thinking that judgment better grounded than judgments justifying the procedures which produced it. And then, without procedural failure, there would be no basis for thinking that any independent standard justified the conclusion that the outcome was unjust. Without an independent standard of justice, one cannot even define the notion of imperfect procedural justice for political outcomes.

The idea that governments, for example, act unjustly, is familiar. However, the question is not whether these judgments are made. It is clear, particularly given the burdens of judgment, that any society without criminal or other sanctions for the expression of opinion will give rise to criticism of the government.[17] Nor is it a question of the content of such judgments, or even their truth-value. It is a matter, again, of the authority on which these judgments rest.

The fact that people hold different opinions is not simply bad luck. Rawls, as already noted, sees it as an inevitable result of exercising judgment in conditions of freedom (Newey 2009). But what goes for reasonable pluralism goes also for the moral authority claimed for judgments. This is so regardless of whether one takes a realist view of these judgments. Suppose a judgment were true, objectively valid, etc. This would still not endow someone who expresses this judgment with authority. By the same token, I do not make an authoritative judgment by saying 'It is raining outside' if I have not checked the weather, even if it happens to be raining outside. Epistemic authority does not relate in a simple way to the truth-value of the judgments one expresses, and nor, *a fortiori*, does political authority.[18]

This is not to say that epistemic factors are irrelevant to determining whether or not a judgment enjoys authority. But where judgments are controversial, it becomes less clear what counts as a source of epistemic authority. People appeal to such a source when in dispute about what to do; when the need for adjudication arises from some unresolved practical question. That is already, potentially, a political question. Moreover, asking whose opinion should count as authoritative unavoidably brings in politics. Given disagreement, the authority question is decided not by who is right, has the strongest arguments, or evidence. Each of these simply raises the authority question again. The question is who can bring about the outcome that their reading of the evidence favours.

To repeat, enjoying such authority is not epistemically normative. The fact that the authority asserts that p is not, in itself, a reason for accepting the truth of p. So Rawls's reasonable pluralism may not be diminished by the presence of authority. Pluralism may well increase, as the authority's reliance on epistemically dubious claims prompts greater probing of them. Earlier it seemed that there could be an independent yardstick for judging political outcomes. But the disagreements arising from the burdens of judgment show this to be illusory, at least in any form that could be of use. This follows from the fact of disagreement, rather than specifically from reasonable disagreement. For there is still a political question to address even if some view were demonstrably unreasonable, given that people disagree about it.

What authority can judgments, which are after all often truth-claims,[19] muster without an agreed method for reaching the truth? Liberal societies committed to free speech sharpen the line between authority and assertibility. Without bars on content, citizens may assert any judgment. But the pluralization of judgments under liberalism inevitably diminishes the authority of particular judgments. This is not simply because there are more of these judgments around, which then suffer the fate of any inflated currency. It is also because when conflicting judgments can circulate freely, each tends to undermine the authority of the rest.[20]

A *conscientious* basis for the judgments fails to establish their authority.[21] They have authority of a kind, namely 'first-person' authority. If a person claims that his conscience tells him to do or think something, this claim is usually indefeasible by others. Persons are treated as authorities on their own consciences, a residue of the 17th-century doctrine of first-person epistemic authority. But, just for this reason, the doctrine says nothing about what happens when one person's conscience conflicts with another's. Each is sovereign in his own sphere, and conscience as such does not obtrude beyond that sphere. First-person authority thus leaves it open what makes public judgments authoritative.[22]

This subject has received considerable attention recently (Rawls 1999). Work has centred on showing how, given private disagreements over judgments of value, liberalism can process judgments asserted and acted on at the public level. Many modern liberals endorse neutrality (Ackerman 1980, Larmore 1987, Barry 1995), the demand that no public judgment should be reasonably rejectable by those it affects. This aims to preclude political decisions favouring one idea of value over others that reasonably reject it. Hence the 'method of avoidance' (Rawls 1999, pp. 375, 434). forswears attempts to decide whose idea of value is right. Instead, it seeks eligibility conditions for judgments grounding public policy, and so to restore authority despite reasonable disagreement. Authority is vested in judgments that survive public contestation conducted with neutral discursive constraints.

Two responses can be made, which are really two sides of one coin. First, it is hard for purely discursive constraints to yield judgments that will be generally received as authoritative. The constraints need a benchmark of reasonableness in deciding what is reasonably rejectable, but this itself lies open to reasonable disagreement. The constraints will foreseeably leave a spillover of judgments, ruled out by the procedure, that some will, not unreasonably, see as not being reasonably rejectable. Second, this constructed notion of public authority is clearly a political *procedure*, on a similar footing to an executive order or vote. Again the idea of a standard independent of procedure proves illusory.

The coin of which these two remarks form opposite sides is a platitude. If a procedure is designed to give authority to all and only the judgments that it has ratified, then judgments will have authority only if they emerge from the procedure. If a judgment acquires authority by having been filtered through the norms of public reason, then it can only be seen as the outcome of a procedure designed to give its outputs authority, by purging them of partisan content. Conversely, if the judgments have by-passed that procedure, they will clearly lack authority. That, again, is the point of the procedure.[23]

So, a specification for imperfect procedural justice could not be met. Truth and authority are distinct. There is no guarantee that any given judgment generated by an authoritative procedure will be true. But there is also no general authoritative standard by which to decide that, say, a certain outcome is unjust, except via the procedures in which authority is reposed. There is a role for expert knowledge in formulating policy or assessing its effects. But expertise only gains authority in the policy process by influencing those who devise and implement it.

There can be no authoritative standard of justice to judge political outcomes, independent of the means for conferring authority via due procedure. Nonetheless, decisions about what norms of justice to pursue, insofar as they are outcome-orientated, will be taken with that outcome in view. It is double-minded to arrive at reasons for settling on a norm such as equality, devise a procedure for generating outcomes that fit the norm, and *then* think that this decision can be ratified by identifying reasons for equality. In Wittgenstein's analogy, it is like buying a second copy of the morning paper to assure oneself that what one has read in the first copy is true (Wittgenstein 1953, §265). This would only have a point if the norm had been picked arbitrarily and reasons then had to be found to support the choice of norm. But a norm of justice itself cannot be arbitrarily chosen, even if, as with lotteries, a just procedure can select an arbitrary outcome.

Pure procedural justice revisited

So is the only stable conception of political justice pure procedural justice? According to that conception, political procedures themselves are the measure of justice, in that their outcomes are *eo ipso* just. Thus political procedures are to be seen on analogy with a lottery that distributes outcomes on a random basis according to a prearranged procedure, such as drawing numbers from a hat. As just noted, this is not to say that the procedures in question are random as those of a lottery are. But like a lottery, any political system of pure procedural justice will itself be the measure of the justice of its outcomes.

In pure procedural justice a distribution is just if it results from the procedure. In principle the procedures can take any form, but procedures will be the only authoritative way to produce outcomes. The procedure can be designed to yield certain outcomes, such as creating distributions to fit a specific template. The procedure will typically include homeostatic devices to achieve the target output, just as thermostats, for instance, are self-corrective mechanisms to keep a system at the target temperature.

Surely, someone may say, something similar is imaginable for political justice. The procedure may be designed to bring about equality in, say, income distribution. Then legislation could lay down that the procedure had been followed if and only if the standard deviation of incomes from a specified point, for example, fell within a certain range. The system will embody pure procedural justice, in that it determines what counts as a just outcome. But the outcomes will not result from a blind application of procedures. Rather the latter will allow, indeed demand, continual adjustments to achieve the target distribution. So actual outcomes are monitored and altered in the light of the procedure's goal.[24]

This is a clear possibility. It arises not just with mechanical devices like servos, but hiring procedures, for example when there is a target quota. Sporting tournaments may be so arranged that certain outcomes are required or are ruled out. But in these examples the outcomes have already been determined as just, or at least as desirable. Some notion of justice may be fed into the system in designing its procedures. Since the procedure is the *measure* of the justice of the outcomes, there is no possibility of challenging them, except on the grounds of their derivation: whether or not they were generated by due process. What is ruled out is mounting an authoritative challenge to a procedurally well-formed outcome on the grounds of its substantive injustice. In that sense, authority has already been built into the system.

This may sound sinisterly authoritarian, even tantamount to thought-control. But these consequences inhere in systems of pure procedural justice. Consider, as an analogy, the metre rod in Paris, as discussed by Kripke (1980).[25] For a time the metre rod was the measure of the standard metre. The metre rod itself determined what measured a metre in length, so there was no question whether the metre rod itself was a metre long. As Kripke argues, however, the rod's significance can be seen as lying in the fact that it 'rigidly' designates the same length across all possible worlds, so that even if the actual rod becomes shorter or longer, the quantity 'one metre' remains invariant. But that is consistent with saying that in the actual world, the rod determines what counts as measuring one metre in length.

Similarly, under pure procedural justice the system for producing just outcomes determines what 'just' is. Justice is what comes out of a non-anomalous running of the system. In the same way, whether something counts as one metre long depends on how it would measure alongside the metre rod. But, just as the rod could have had a different length, the fact that the procedures' outputs fix what counts as just does not rule it out that a different set of procedures could have operated, whose outputs would then have embodied justice in their turn. And then the reference of 'is just' might have differed from the actual world.

A further objection now looms, suggested by Kripke's interpretation of the metre rod example. In pure procedural justice, the procedure fixes the reference of 'just', as applied to its outcomes. But precisely for that reason, it does not follow that actual outcomes will be just when measured by the standard that the procedures exist to realize.[26] In the same way, given that the locution 'one metre' designates rigidly, the actual measuring device the standard metre rod in Paris may in some circumstances fail to measure one metre. So, someone may say, 'is just' may not be predicable of the procedures' outcomes, when judged against the standard for which the procedures were devised. So even a system of pure procedural justice cannot tie the standard of justice indissolubly to the procedures.

The short answer is that if the system is one of pure procedural justice, then its outputs by definition cannot be at odds with justice, as long as the procedures have been followed. The objection is really that no procedure *can* embody justice in this way. That would certainly help to explain why justice provokes disagreement: any claim to have captured it definitively in a procedure must fail, as one can always intelligibly object that an outcome is unjust. If so, attempts to implement justice politically via a system of pure procedural justice fail. They fix a reference for 'is just' which no actual procedures can infallibly track. This is essentially the epistemic realist objection to conventionalism: that there is a real external standard that the convention may breach. It underlies Dworkin's insistence that there is a 'right answer' to disputed questions of jurisprudence (Dworkin 1977). If so, judicial constructions of statute may simply miss the mark. The judges' decision cannot in that sense be final. But then we return to imperfect procedural justice, which foundered on the lack of authority for objections to specific outcomes.

We have reached an apparent impasse. The three versions of procedural justice have all proven inadequate. Perfect procedural justice rests on double-mindedness about independent standards of justice: a procedure will be 'right' only if it fits a political decision to bring about a certain outcome. Its imperfect procedural counterpart succumbs to the lack of an authoritative independent standard by which to judge the procedure's outcomes. Pure procedural justice, as we have just seen, falls foul of the fact that conventions about justice can be challenged, even on a stipulative view of the conventions. If the procedures implicitly fix the reference of 'is just', then it always remains possible to claim that some specific procedural outcome is unjust.

Perfect and imperfect procedural justice are hobbled by the lack of a true external source of authority for judgments of justice; their 'pure' counterpart, by the lack of an authoritative internal basis for such judgments. That gives grounds for thinking that debate over justice may be interminable.[27]

Conclusion

The argument set out above could be thought to be about *legitimacy* rather than justice.[28] It accepts that individuals may reject the outcomes of the political process. In doing so, they may well think that the outcome is unjust; but the modified form of the argument states perhaps they will not conclude from this that the outcome is illegitimate. They may accept that the procedures that led to it were duly followed, and that the procedures themselves were legitimate, while still regarding it as unjust. Nor, conversely, does the claim that the outcome was legitimate entail that it was just.

Even under pure procedural justice, valid outcomes may be unjust. For that reason, someone can say that an outcome is unjust, while also accepting its procedural legitimacy. If so, paradox seems to loom. In pure procedural justice, it may be that:

(1) the procedures have been followed correctly in respect of a certain outcome, R;
(2) if the procedures have been followed correctly in respect of an outcome, then that outcome is just.

So,

(3) R is just.

However,

(4) R is unjust.

One obvious response is to argue that one can *regard* outcomes as unjust, even though they are not. Another sidestep, as noted, is to recast procedural justice in terms of legitimacy, so that outcomes may be legitimate without being just. But the lesson from the discussion of pure procedural justice is that these moves are not forced. Even under pure proceduralism, one need not insist that the procedures' results are just: that is, one rejects 3, because one rejects 2, since even procedurally unimpeachable outcomes can be unjust. That leaves room for dispute about justice – the sort of dispute that is the stuff of politics.[29] It follows that politics, including political dispute over justice, cannot be foreclosed by due procedure. Equally, it cannot be foreclosed by a theoretical construction.

Do liberal democracies have politics that are just, or just politics? One might say: both and neither. I have suggested that pure proceduralism offers the only stable version of Rawls's three forms of procedural justice, precisely because it is, at some level, decisionistic. However, scope also remains, by stepping outside procedure, to query the justice of specific outcomes. Conversely, dissentients can insist that another procedure would have forestalled *this* unjust outcome. That does not mean that there is any procedure that is incapable of yielding unjust outcomes. It does suggest that politics abides, both in the unavoidability of procedures, and in their implacable open-endedness.

Acknowledgments

This paper was given at the University of Gdansk in May 2010 as part of a conference on political realism. I warmly thank the organizers, Artur Szutta and Natasza Szutta, for their hospitality and for the invitation to speak; and John Horton for setting up the invitation.

Notes

1. For present purposes, I take 'politics' as shorthand for a set of procedurally mediated actions that generate public policy outcomes. This is not intended to define 'politics' (Newey 2001, ch. 2).
2. Saint-Simon is often claimed to have inspired this remark.
3. There is the further argument that justice itself is eliminated if conflict is removed (Hampshire 1999).
4. As I explain below, this is not to say that no such judgment is possible. The question rather concerns the *authority* that such judgments enjoy given political disagreement over what to do.
5. Conscientious refusal differs from civil disobedience in that it involves refusal of a requirement issued by the state such as conscription without necessarily calling for a change in the law, and without using law-breaking (beyond the fact of refusal itself) as an essential means to achieve that end.
6. That is, an account of the norms that shape basic political institutions, procedures and (maybe) outcomes (Newey 2001, Introduction).
7. For a thorough examination of these as competing distributive principles, see Miller (2001).
8. A further point is that since there are different interpretations of equality, it will be a real question – a political one – which to implement in this situation. Achieving equality in one respect will mean failing to achieve it in another (Geuss 2008).
9. To this extent the standard of justice resembles truth, seen as a property derived in formal systems via theorems. But theorems can be intuitively true, but not provable within the system. Then it seems that what is derivable may not be untrue (so the system is inconsistent) or it is true but not derivable (so it is incomplete). Parallel possibilities exist for systems of justice.
10. '[T]he basic structure is a case of imperfect procedural justice' (Rawls 1971, p. 89).
11. Consider the 2000 US Presidential Election, decided by the Federal Supreme Court. The court ruled that the methods for counting disputed ballots in Florida violated the Equal Protection clause of the Fourteenth Amendment. Meanwhile, critics maintained that the treatment of the Floridean ballots effectively disenfranchised voters in some counties. This example shows the difficulty not only of providing authoritative judgments about justice, but also for determining whether even the *procedures* have been upheld.
12. Or at least not unreasonable: presumably the burdens of judgment mean that the burden of proof falls on those who claim that a dissenting opinion is unreasonable.
13. '[A] theory of civil disobedience […] is designed only for the special case of a nearly just society […] in which some serious violations of justice nevertheless do occur' (Rawls (1971, p. 363).
14. Emanuela Ceva points out that there may be considerations independent of justice that allow for the evaluation of procedural outcomes (Ceva 2009). For an opposing view, see Rossi (2009).

15. See Sen (2009) and John Horton's paper in this issue. I am also indebted to Bruce Haddock for raising this point in discussion.
16. I cast doubt elsewhere on whether the burdens of judgment really warrant reasonable pluralism (Newey 2009).
17. As Rawls (1996, pp. 37, 54–58) indicates, divergent judgments are the foreseeable effect of shouldering the burdens in conditions of freedom.
18. I treat a source *S* as an authority for person *A* if I take the fact that *S* asserts *p* as a *pro tanto* reason for *A*'s accepting *p*.
19. This requires only the applicability of the truth-predicate to the relevant judgment, which remains consistent with, for example, a deflationary account of truth (Blackburn 2005, e.g. chs 3, 5).
20. As Hume notes in the *Treatise of Human Nature*, Bk 1, Pt 4, ch. 2, §12 (Hume 1978).
21. The appeal to conscience was historically prominent in defences of free speech (Walwyn 1989, pp. 433–445).
22. Hobbes argues in *Leviathan*, ch. 42, that it is *because* of first-person authority in matters of conscience that the civil power can act repressively in matters of religion (Hobbes 1996, pp. 343–344).
23. Truth is closed under entailment. But the parallel does not hold for justice and procedure. Just starting-points need not yield just outcomes under just procedure. This is important to G. A. Cohen's critique of Robert Nozick's transactional theory of justice, which treats justice as truthlike in this respect.
24. Sen (2009), for example, may have something like this in mind when distinguishing between justice as 'transcendental institutionalism' and as 'realization-focused comparison'.
25. Kripke (1980, p. 48) argues that '1 metre' is a rigid designator, i.e. a locution that designates the same thing in all possible worlds (and in particular, the same length). It is therefore a contingent *a priori* truth for Kripke, since although the metre rod fixes the reference of the length '1 metre', that rod could have had a different length.
26. This point is central in the political and legal philosophy of Ronald Dworkin (Dworkin 1986).
27. Though not necessarily 'rationally' interminable, in Alasdair MacIntyre's sense (MacIntyre 1988).
28. I owe this suggestion to John Horton.
29. This does not assume a definition of 'politics', e.g. as essentially 'agonistic'. It assumes only that politics is practical, and what is to be done is often not practically determinate, so that it is a *potential* subject of dispute. This point is sometimes not grasped by 'realists' as well as their liberal adversaries (e.g. Mouffe 2005).

References

Ackerman, B., 1980. *Social justice in the liberal state.* New Haven, CT: Yale University Press.

Barry, B., 1995. *Justice as impartiality*. Oxford: Clarendon.
Bedau, H. A., ed., 1991. *Civil disobedience in focus*. London: Routledge.
Blackburn, S., 2005. *Truth*. Oxford: Oxford University Press.
Ceva, E., 2009. Just procedures with controversial outcomes: on the grounds for substantive disputation with a procedural theory of justice. *Res Publica*, 15, 219–235.
Dworkin, R., 1977. *Taking rights seriously*. London: Duckworth.
Dworkin, R., 1986. *Law's empire*. London: Fontana.
Engels, F., 1975. *Socialism: utopian and scientific*. New York, NY: International Books.
Geuss, R., 2008. *Philosophy and real politics*. Princeton, NJ: Princeton University Press.
Hampshire, S., 1999. *Justice is conflict*. Princeton, NJ: Princeton University Press.
Hobbes, T., 1996. *Leviathan*. Revd edn. Cambridge: Cambridge University Press.
Hume, D., 1978. *Treatise of human nature*. Oxford: Clarendon.
Kierkegaard, S., 1985. *Fear and trembling; dialectical lyric by Johannes de Silentio*. London: Harmondsworth.
Kripke, S., 1980. *Naming and necessity*. Cambridge, MA: Harvard University Press.
Larmore, C., 1987. *Patterns of moral complexity*. Cambridge: Cambridge University Press.
MacIntyre, A., 1988. *Whose justice? Which rationality?* London: Duckworth.
Miller, D., 2001. *Principles of social justice*. Cambridge, MA: Harvard University Press.
Mouffe, C., 2005. *The return of the political*. Revd ed. London: Verso.
Newey, G., 2001. *After politics: the rejection of politics in contemporary liberal philosophy*. London: Palgrave.
Newey, G., 2009. John Rawls: liberalism at the limits of intolerance. *In*: S. P. Young, ed. *Reflections on Rawls: an assessment of his legacy*. Aldershot: Ashgate, 131–152.
Rawls, J., 1971. *A theory of justice*. Oxford: Oxford University Press.
Rawls, J., 1996. *Political liberalism*. New York, NY: Columbia University Press.
Rawls, J., 1999. *Collected papers*. Cambridge, MA: Harvard University Press.
Rossi, E., 2009. The exemption that confirms the rule: reflections on proceduralism and the UK hybrid embryos controversy. *Res Publica*, 15, 237–250.
Scanlon, T. M., 1998. *What we owe to each other*. Cambridge, MA: Belknap.
Sen, A., 2009. *The idea of justice*. London: Harmondsworth.
Skinner, Q., 2002. *Visions of politics*. Vol. 1. Cambridge: Cambridge University Press.
Walwyn, W., 1989. Juries justified. *In*: J. R. MacMichael and B. Taft, eds. *The writings of William Walwyn*. Athens, GA: University of Georgia Press.
Wittgenstein, L., 1953. *Philosophical investigations*. Oxford: Blackwell.

Beyond legitimacy. Can proceduralism say anything relevant about justice?

Emanuela Ceva

Department of Political and Social Sciences, University of Pavia, Pavia, Italy

Whilst legitimacy is often thought to concern the *processes* through which coercive decisions are made in society, justice has been standardly viewed as a 'substantial' matter concerning the moral justification of the terms of social cooperation. Accordingly, theorization about procedures may seem appropriate for the former but not for the latter. To defend proceduralism as a relevant approach to justice, I distinguish three questions: (1) Who is entitled to exercise coercive power? (2) On what terms should the participants to a scheme of cooperation interact? (3) How should the costs and benefits produced by cooperation be distributed? Legitimacy concerns (1), whereas justice applies to (2) and (3). Although the appropriateness of proceduralism is debatable in relation to (3), it seems well equipped to address the justice-related question in (2). And it does so by focusing on the inherent moral acceptability of the way in which persons are treated by the procedures through which they interact.

Introductory

Can the procedures through which a society is structured be considered as inherently valuable as just? Or is justice to be thought to reside in their outcomes, to the achievement of which procedures are merely subservient? This paper takes issue with the widespread wariness of proceduralism as a justice-relevant approach to normativity. Interestingly, such a generalized disregard of the inherent value of procedures in matters of justice does not seem to be matched by an equal lack of interest when the normative regard, as it were, moves from the justice of a polity to its legitimacy. Indeed, a number of studies defend procedural approaches to legitimacy, especially when it comes to accounting for the justification of authority in a democracy (for example, Christiano 1996, Peter 2008, Waldron 1999).

The thought underlying such a double attitude towards proceduralism may be summarized as follows: whilst legitimacy has to do with the *processes* through which coercive political decisions are made, justice is more a 'substantial' matter concerning the moral justification of the terms of social cooperation, against which the qualities of the decisions made by those who have the authority to make them are to be evaluated (Rawls 1993, pp. 427–429; for a discussion, see Hinsch 2010). Accordingly, the argument goes, theorization about procedures seems to be more appropriate for issues of legitimacy than for those of justice.

I contend that this argument is inaccurate for it mixes three different levels of analysis: (1) Who is entitled to exercise coercive power in society? (2) On what terms should the participants to a scheme of social cooperation interact? (3) How should the costs and benefits produced by social cooperation be distributed? I argue that considerations of legitimacy apply to level (1), whereas considerations of justice apply to levels (2) and (3). Although, as I shall try to show in line with many critics of proceduralism, the appropriateness of a procedural approach to the justice-related question in (3) is debatable, proceduralism seems well equipped to provide a sound answer to the, equally justice-related, question in (2). It does so by focusing on the way in which persons should be treated by the procedures through which they interact in society, once all issues of entitlement in the use of power are set (1) and independently of the outcomes of the interaction (3).

In what follows, I start by briefly outlining what is generally presented as a standard account of proceduralism, drawing on John Rawls's sketch of perfect, imperfect and pure procedural justice. I then distinguish four senses in which pure proceduralism (the idea that valuable procedures lead to valuable outcomes) may be relevant for issues of justice and legitimacy: two of these are to be found in the uses made by Rawls (1971) of the idea of pure procedural justice, respectively, as a method for the justification of principles of justice (constructivism) and as characterizing a society's basic structure (background procedural justice); the third sense, concerning the characterization of the kinds of prescription principles of justice should make, is illustrated through reference to the work of Stuart Hampshire (Hampshire 1999); the fourth may be found in procedural theories of democracy and concerns the sources of authority of collective decisions. Such four senses are not always well distinguished in the literature and this certainly does not help in an accurate assessment of the merits and limits of proceduralism.

With these specifications in place, I move on to presenting the most common lines of criticism addressed against pure proceduralism. To do so, I rehearse an argument presented by William Nelson (Nelson 1980) that pure proceduralism is better understood as a theory of entitlements playing a descriptive – but not a normative – function in accounting for what goes on in just transactions. After taking, and in fact lending support to, Nelson's point regarding pure procedural accounts of justice and legitimacy,

I argue that a distinctive fruitful role for proceduralism may be preserved if we divorce the idea that the interesting point of having just procedures is their capacity of leading to just outcomes and we recognize procedures as an independent *locus* for justice in its own right. Procedural principles of justice would therefore prescribe how the interaction between citizens in society should be structured for it to be inherently morally justifiable to them. Proceduralism is thus presented as a complement to outcome theories of justice, not as an alternative to them. In so doing, I hope my analysis will hit the target of offering an analytically accurate re-orientation of the debate about the possible approaches through which the justice and the legitimacy of a society should be assessed.

Before proceeding, two brief but important preliminary clarifications are in order. First, I make reference to the debate on normative, rather than descriptive, legitimacy but I am not interested in testing the cogency of any one specific normative conception. Accordingly, I base my considerations on a distinction between the *concepts* of legitimacy and justice and consider proceduralism as a possible connotation the concept of justice may take, without committing myself to defending any specific *conception*.

Second, in this paper I do not contrast proceduralism with 'substantivism', as has almost always been the case in the literature.[1] This use of the terms suggests that whilst outcomes have to do with substance, procedures are a 'mere' formal matter. But this seems wrong, for we can certainly speak of outcomes in formal terms (as in 'every person X should get an equal share of the good Y') and of procedures in substantial terms (as in 'every minority cultural group should out of respect be given a veto power during deliberation on all decisions which have a direct impact on them').[2] What really distinguishes proceduralism is not its giving more formal (and less substantial) normative prescriptions, but its normative focus on the inherent qualities of procedures rather than on those of outcomes. Accordingly I contrast procedural theories with what I call – mostly for lack of a better term – 'outcome theories'.

The standard characterization of proceduralism

In order to make sense of the neglect of proceduralism as a relevant take on justice, it is useful to retrace its origins in the infamous distinction theorized by Rawls between perfect, imperfect and pure proceduralism (Rawls 1971, pp. 85–86). In the cases of perfect and imperfect proceduralism, the property qualifying outcomes as inherently just is established before – and independently of – the construction and application of the procedures to deliver them. On perfect proceduralist accounts, procedures should be capable of leading to the desired outcome with certainty. For imperfect proceduralism, instead, there is no guarantee that a specific procedure to reach an inherently just outcome can actually be devised. The example Rawls suggests to illustrate imperfect proceduralism is that of a criminal trial:

> The desired outcome is that the defendant should be declared guilty if and only if he has committed the offence with which he is charged. The trial procedure is framed to search for and to establish the truth in this regard. But it seems impossible to design the legal rules so that they always lead to the correct result. (Rawls 1971, p. 85)

These versions of proceduralism are distinguished from what Rawls calls pure procedural justice. On this account, the qualities of a just outcome cannot be known before a just procedure is actually carried out and in fact the justice of outcomes depends entirely on the justice of procedures leading to them. Rawls thinks that such an account of proceduralism is that at work, for instance, in gambling: 'if a number of persons engage in a series of fair bets, the distribution of cash after the last bet is fair, or at least not unfair, whatever the distribution is' (Rawls 1971, p. 86).

In sum, in the case of im/perfect proceduralism, justice is an exclusive attribute of outcomes to attain which procedures are merely subservient. In the case of pure proceduralism, instead, no constraints are placed on the acceptability of a certain outcome except the correct application of the procedure leading to it. Procedures acquire, thus, a central role in the articulation of a concept of justice as they are thought to be capable, if correctly carried out, of transferring their properties to their outcomes. This latter seems to be the only genuine account of proceduralism offered by Rawls and, therefore, my subsequent analysis will focus on this.

Proceduralism about what?

This characterization of proceduralism is however too formal to tell us anything about whether it is a fruitful approach to justice at all. The examples given by Rawls are not helpful as they are meant to be purely illustrative of the kinds of reasoning that proceduralism requires. In particular, on consideration of their heterogeneity, they do not tell us much in terms of the kinds of issue for which pure proceduralism may be relevant or the normative function it could play. So, in what sense may a theory be purely procedural?

A first sense in which a theory may be purely procedural has regard to the way in which principles of justice are justified. Here, proceduralism reads constructivism. For example, according to Rawls, just principles are those that rational agents would choose through a certain process (the original position) and under certain conditions (the veil of ignorance). The correctness of the principles of justice is not derived from their corresponding to a prior moral order, but from their being 'constructed' through a procedure structured in compliance with the fundamental principles of practical reasoning (Rawls 1971, p. 120). This account qualifies constructivism as an instance of pure proceduralism: relevant outcomes are justified as they are constructed through a procedure displaying certain inherent qualities. This understanding of proceduralism as constructivism, however, is not that in which I am most interested in this paper as it is pitched at a meta-ethical level which is not – as will become apparent – that at which I think it is more fruitful to defend against a general scepticism the importance and the interest of a procedural account of justice as disjunct from one of legitimacy. So I shall set it aside with no further argument.

A second sense in which the idea of pure proceduralism is at work in Rawls's theory qualifies what Rawls calls 'background procedural justice': the idea that once a just political constitution underpinning a just system of cooperation between citizens is in place, whatever specific distribution of goods is achieved would be acceptable to all. In Rawls's words 'in this kind of procedural justice the *correctness* of the distribution is founded on the *justice* of the scheme of cooperation from which it arises' (Rawls 1971, p. 88; emphasis added). Although this article is not intended as an exercise in Rawlsian scholarship, I would like to raise a brief point on this use of the idea of pure procedural justice. Rawls seems to say that once justice is secured at the background level whatever happens is acceptable. Also, he seems to be persuaded that it would be acceptable as *just*. But is this use of the attribute 'just' coherent with Rawls's own position that justice is the first virtue of political and social institutions and its appropriate domain is a society's basic structure? I sense it would be more accurate to say that once justice is secured at the background level, whatever happens is acceptable as it does not raise any issue of justice, for all such issues have already been addressed at a more fundamental level (such a reading would account for the different terminology used in Rawls's original formulation of the argument, as quoted above, in which the distributive outcomes of a just basic structure are defined simply as *correct*).

If this account is plausible, then the idea of procedural justice would do little normative work but simply be a device for presenting the idea that background justice (the justice of institutions) has priority over distributive justice (the justice of individual transactions within the institutional framework). But background justice itself is not purely procedural. Although Rawls's principles of justice do not offer prescriptions to make sure the outcomes of individual transactions are commensurate to individuals' specific desires and needs, they connote morally acceptable distributive outcomes of social primary goods (including basic liberties and opportunities). Moreover, the qualities of the rules constituting a society's basic structure are designed to attain distributive outcomes that, whatever their dimensions, display certain inherently valuable qualities in terms of the containment of acceptable inequalities. Sketchy as they are, such considerations are enough to suggest that the idea of pure proceduralism plays quite normatively weak a role in Rawls's conception of justice.

A third sense in which a theory of justice may be purely procedural can be deduced by looking at the kinds of prescription principles of justice contain, whether they characterize the terms or the outcomes of social cooperation. Most accounts of distributive justice address the latter concern: principles of justice are meant to adjudicate between citizens' competing claims on certain goods so that each citizen receives her fair share of the goods at stake. When justice is conceived in these terms, theorization about procedures does not seem to be relevant in its own right but only as an instrument to bringing about a desired, inherently just distributive outcome. Although this position has dominated by and large the thinking of justice-driven political philosophers, a few exceptions are well in place. Among such exceptions one should mention at least Hampshire (1999). According to Hampshire, conflicts about the properties of distributive outcomes are ineliminable in politics. The most political philosophers can do is to suggest peaceful means to contain such conflicts. Hampshire sets this task for political philosophers as he is persuaded that despite the persistence of disagreement about the justice of certain distributive outcomes, every person recognizes anarchy as derived from violent means of dealing with conflicts as a great political evil to avoid (Hampshire 1999, pp. 77–78, 90–91). Accordingly, political institutions should make sure they provide procedures through which such conflicts may be kept peacefully at bay.

Hampshire thinks that no normative creative effort is needed to characterize such procedures because almost all societies are already equipped – and have been traditionally so equipped – with the procedural instruments they need. Such instruments should be found in procedures of adversary argumentation – which command that all sides in a conflict be heard – with which everyone is familiar from practice both in their polities and in their personal reasoning (Hampshire 1999, pp. 33, 58). When couched in these terms the idea of justice seems to get quite close to that of legitimacy. After all, the requirement that all sides in a conflict be heard can be read as the expression of a commitment to making sure that the authority to decide over a conflictual issue is distributed evenly between all relevant parties, so that no one can prevail unduly over the others.[3]

Such a hint leads us to the fourth sense in which pure proceduralism may be employed in normative theorizing, by shifting the attention from questions of justice to those of legitimacy. As suggested, the domain of legitimacy concerns the ownership and exercise of political authority, where authority standardly means the right to rule: the right to issue binding commands and to enforce them through coercive power.[4] The domain of justice concerns, instead, the subject matter over which legitimate authority can be exercised. Theorization about justice concerns, in other words, the justification of the terms and conditions of social cooperation, that is the moral acceptability of the way in which a society is organized and the costs and benefits of cooperation are distributed.[5]

Because the way in which a society is organized has been standardly viewed as instrumental to reaching a morally acceptable distribution of the costs and benefits of cooperation, justice has been standardly thought to reside in outcomes rather than in procedures. On the other hand, as political authority is exercised through making politically binding decisions, legitimacy has often (though not standardly)[6] been viewed as a property of the procedures through which decision-making processes are articulated. From this perspective, defended by a number of theorists of democracy, legitimate procedures, if correctly applied, lead to legitimate decisions, whatever they happen to be (Christiano 1996, Dahl 1956, Peter 2008, Waldron 1999).

As a result of such a clarificatory journey through accounts of proceduralism, we are left with the following positions. On the one hand, justice-driven political philosophers have resorted to the idea of pure procedural justice in any of the three following senses: (1) to describe meta-ethical reasoning about the justice of social cooperation; (2) to draw attention to the norms on which social cooperation is based rather than to the contingent outcomes of specific transactions; and (3) to propose an account of what holds societies together, given the impossibility of reaching consensus on distributive outcomes. On the other hand, proceduralism has been frequently adopted by legitimacy-driven theorists to account for the sources of political authority in collective decision-making. With such specifications on the table regarding the subject matters of proceduralism, we can move on to assessing its normative cogency.

Legitimacy and the 'standard' critique of proceduralism

William Nelson offered one of the most focused critiques of proceduralism. In discussing Rawls's take on pure proceduralism, Nelson (1980) distinguishes two senses in which it might be considered: a weak interpretation and a strong one. According to the former, proceduralism plays only a classification function: it helps us to reach a correct description of what goes on in certain situations. According to the latter, proceduralism is taken to play an explanatory function: it offers an account of why certain outcomes are considered just in certain situations (Nelson 1980, p. 506).

In assessing the normative cogency of the strong interpretation, Nelson believes that defenders of pure proceduralism are at trouble to explain what the property is, possession of which by a procedure ensures the justice of its outcome. For Nelson (1980, p. 507), to account for such a property, pure proceduralists' arguments are doomed either to boil down to some voluntaristic theory of entitlement (by considering whether the persons involved in the procedure act freely and are entitled to what they exchange) or to im/perfect proceduralism (by calling in a procedure-independent criterion to evaluate the justice of the outcome).

So, if supporters of strong proceduralism want to keep their distance from im/perfect formulations, they must admit that their theories in fact mimic voluntary theories of entitlement. Nelson's idea goes as follows: consider the case of an exchange, in which 'if you want my bicycle we bargain and I agree to sell it to you for $50, the result of the exchange is just'. Now, according to Nelson,

> what we have in the [case] described is people voluntarily exercising their rights. If it is my bicycle, I have a certain range of discretionary authority over it. This discretionary authority includes the authority to transfer ownership to someone else on mutually agreeable terms [...] of course I must really have the right in question: I cannot have stolen the bicycle and there must be no force or fraud. But if such conditions are met, the outcome is just. (Nelson 1980, p. 505)

If this account holds, for Nelson, we can still go on *describing* such a situation as one of pure procedural justice and, thus, remain faithful to proceduralism in its weak interpretation. But the truth of pure procedural justice in its strong interpretation would be seriously undermined as its explanatory function would fail: what does the normative work in explaining the justice of the outcome is not a specific property of the procedure but the condition that the principle of voluntary entitlements be respected.

Such a translation of proceduralism into terms of an entitlement theory, drives it closer to matters of legitimacy rather than justice. Recall the definition of legitimacy as responding to the question about who is entitled to exercise coercive power in society. Recall also the characterization of legitimacy as a property of the procedures through which decision-making processes are articulated so that legitimate procedures, if correctly applied, lead to legitimate decisions, whatever they happen to be. On what I take to be a fairly standard account of democratic legitimacy, if everyone who is entitled to have a say on the matter at stake has been granted an equal chance to do so, then the results of the deliberation would be regarded as morally authoritative. This is due to everyone's having contributed to the determination of the result, quite apart from whether they all agree with it on the grounds of their different criteria of outcome justice. Justice is thus considered here a distinctively outcome-concerned matter, and legitimacy – as a theory of who is entitled to exercise authority – may be *described* in procedural terms.

The idea that theories of legitimacy may be expressed in terms of theories of entitlement is certainly verified on typically contractualist views of legitimacy, developed following John Locke's footsteps. As is well known, Locke thinks that all individuals possess equal political authority in the state of nature. However, natural law is too indeterminate to constitute the backbone of society. Moreover, in the state of nature, people have no instruments to sanction violations of the natural law. Therefore, it is rational for individuals to enter a social contract transferring their political authority to the civil state which is entrusted with the power to instantiate the natural law and sanction its violations. The authority of the civil state to do so is legitimate if the transfer of authority from the individuals to the state has happened in the right way, through each individual's uncoerced consent (Locke [1690] 1990). Such an account of legitimacy is procedural *qua* historical: it derives legitimacy from the process through which people transfer their entitlements.

As anticipated, for Nelson, apparent instances of proceduralism of this sort may be straightforwardly translated into the currency of the free exercise of entitlement. If I own a certain good, I can exercise discretionary authority over it, including that of transferring ownership to another person. Analogously, if I have a range of discretionary authority over the determination of the rules to which I should conform and I transfer (portions of) my authority to someone else, this person will be entitled to make decisions for me on the rules that should govern me and I shall be bound by such rules as legitimate. On this interpretation, legitimacy would belong to the realm of Nelson's weak proceduralism as describing correctly how those who are entitled to exercise authority exercise it during decision-making.

Rescuing proceduralism about justice from neglect

Is this really all the work proceduralism can do? Is its only function to describe in an intelligible form the workings of a theory of entitlements in legitimacy-related matters? I do not think so and to make my case I propose to look at proceduralism differently: as a theory advocating the importance of the way in which persons are treated by the procedures through which their scheme of cooperation is articulated as a proper *locus* of justice.

What all discussions of proceduralism (except the present) seem to share is the belief that its appeal (or the lack thereof) consists in the idea that even if we disagree on outcomes, we can nonetheless reach an agreement on procedures and that if we manage to do so just procedures will yield just outcomes. This is the idea of proceduralism at the heart of Rawls's and Hampshire's accounts presented above. But this account of the 'merits' of proceduralism has two major flaws. First, the idea that an agreement on the properties qualifying just procedures is easier to reach than one on those qualifying just outcomes is debatable. As argued elsewhere, if disagreement on values is acknowledged, it seems unsound to hold expectations that it will not also affect the properties qualifying just procedures, besides those qualifying just outcomes (Cohen 1994, Rawls 1993, Ceva 2007). Think as an example of the disputes revolving around what decision-making procedures would be more just in a liberal democracy, whether they should be majority voting procedures or procedures of unanimous deliberation through discourse. Secondly, outcomes and procedures are two distinct social and political objects: why should the criteria that apply to the qualities of the one tell us something about those of the other? Episodes of contestation, including acts of civil disobedience, in a democracy seem to show quite clearly that even when people agree on the virtues of the decision-making process they are no less likely to find it wrong to comply with its outcome should it clash with their ideas of what is morally right.

This idea is nicely captured in the following burlesque account of proceduralism discussed by Martha Nussbaum:

> it seems to the outcome-oriented theorist as if a cook has a fancy, sophisticated pasta-maker, and assures her guests that the pasta made in this machine will be by definition good, since it is the best machine on the market. But surely, the outcome theorist says, the guests want to taste the pasta and see for themselves. (Nussbaum 2006, p. 83)

Despite being simplistic, Nussbaum's example seems to be well-targeted at those accounts of pure proceduralism, which are adamant that procedures are capable of transferring their properties to their outcomes.[7] But this is as far as it goes. There is at least another independent claim about proceduralism in matters of justice which remains beyond Nussbaum's critical target: that procedures (as well as outcomes) may be *loci* of justice for quite distinct reasons and in accordance with quite different standards from those employed to evaluate the qualities of outcomes. Crudely put, in assessing the moral acceptability of the terms and conditions of social cooperation (the domain of justice), what matters is not only what people get, but also how they get it. Such a reasoning does not apply to any procedure we can think of: certain procedures in society are indeed adopted only as instruments to produce outcomes (just as the raison d'être of the pasta maker is to make good pasta). But this does not imply that all procedures in society have mere instrumental value.

Consider, as an example, the principle of due process in legal proceedings. The importance attributed to such a principle has quite standardly been viewed as an instance of either epistemic proceduralism or imperfect procedural justice (see, respectively, Estlund 2007, and Rawls 1971): the features of due process allow for the truth of facts to be restored and are thus instrumental to making sure that the defendant be declared guilty only if she has actually committed the crime. However, it seems inaccurate to say that this outcome-oriented account exhausts the reasons for valuing the principle of due process. Besides their instrumental role in leading to the final verdict, the procedures according to which the prosecutor and defence attorney interact, the room given to each of them to make their cases and the terms according to which these are made are endowed with intrinsic value and may constitute an object of autonomous theorizing.

My main claim here is that even if the verdict is just (the person declared guilty has in fact committed the crime and been given the right punishment), the process leading to it might have been unjust (the defendant has been treated in a morally unacceptable way, e.g. she was threatened to get a confession). This does not make the outcome unjust, but some kind of relevant injustice has nonetheless occurred. And, if we turn a blind eye to the inherent qualities of procedures or we consider them only in outcome-related terms, we might not be able to detect it. So, unlike Wojciech Sadurski (1984), I think that it is true that '[d]ue process is a necessary, but not sufficient condition for just treatment' (Resnick 1977, p. 213). However, I do not think so in the sense that procedural constraints are a necessary but not sufficient condition for the justice of outcomes. I think it true rather in the sense that bringing about justice in procedures is a necessary but not sufficient condition to bring about justice in society (or in legal courts). In this sense, proceduralism as I see it is not an alternative to outcome theories. They are better understood if conceived as quite distinct approaches to dealing with different demands of justice. Specifically, if – as suggested – theorization about justice concerns the justification of the terms and conditions of social cooperation, a double test of moral acceptability is in order concerning both the procedures through which a society is organized *and* the distribution of the costs and benefits of social cooperation among citizens (also Griffin 2003).[8]

This reading allows responding in a different way to Nelson's challenge to the novelty of proceduralism. Its main contribution is not to propose a novel criterion to evaluate the justice of outcomes, but to point to a different justice-relevant *locus*: that of the inherent properties of the procedures through which citizens interact. So, to probe the cogency of proceduralism, one should not enquire, as Nelson put it, how a procedure having a certain property may yield just results. The appropriate question to ask is rather what property a procedure should display to be just per se. On this view, and to wrap it all up in a slogan, according to this understanding of proceduralism justice is not a product of procedures, but is (also) found in procedures.

For this account of proceduralism to be normatively cogent, one cannot simply argue that, for a procedure to be just, it must enjoy the *de facto* acceptance of the parties. As argued elsewhere (Ceva 2009), normative work is necessary to single out the property, possession of which makes procedures morally acceptable to those who are expected to interact through them (Miller 1999, p. 103). To put it in the parlance employed throughout this article, unlike matters of legitimacy, justice cannot and should not be reduced to considerations of voluntary transfer of entitlements. As already explained, on an actual consent account of legitimacy, if I voluntarily transfer to a third party my authority to decide on the constraints that should be imposed on my conduct, such a third party will be legitimated to exercise coercive power over me. Such a situation may be *described*, following Nelson's suggestion, as one of pure proceduralism: whatever those who retain authority will command (outcome) will be legitimate as they are entitled to issue such a command by virtue of my having voluntarily transferred to them the power to do so (procedure). Justice is a different matter. It is not enough for me to have *actually* consented to x to make x just as, in order for this to be the case, a further step is necessary: x must be morally acceptable to me according to an appropriately devised test of justification capable of bringing out justice-relevant considerations and tempering the influence of morally irrelevant contingencies which might instead have an impact on my actual consent (this is the main idea underpinning Rawls's original position).[9]

The point can be fleshed out further through reference to games which are often taken to be an instance of proceduralism, or, in fact, of pure procedural justice. As much as the idea of pure proceduralism can be used to describe why the outcomes of rules-governed games are acceptable (see Rawls's example of gambling), I would resist invoking justice at all in such scenarios. Similarly to what was argued above, what does the normative work in a game is the *voluntariness* of the players' acceptance of and compliance with the rules which define the game as it is. Whatever rules the players decide to abide by define the game and are considered an appropriate way to establish the acceptability of the outcome of that game, quite apart from the moral qualities inherent in such rules (Arneson 1993, p. 129, Sadurski 1984, p. 348). Consider as an example the variety of rules articulating fighting games, ranging from Greek–Roman wrestling (to which widely recognizable rules of fair play apply) to Mixed Martial Arts (where minimal rules apply to fights involving a variety of more or less cruel techniques). However, the fact that certain rules, as crazy as they might be, are *de facto* voluntarily accepted by a bunch of people hardly tells us anything normatively relevant about the justice of such rules (or of their outcomes). It seems quite plausible to say that breaking the rules of a game is wrong not as that would be unjust, in any meaningful sense of violating what morality requires, but as it would be inappropriate for the kind of game one is playing.

Accordingly, on my proposed account, the reasons to prefer one specific procedure to another are not to be found in its being *de facto* and freely accepted by those who interact through it; nor are they to be sought in its capacity to produce just outcomes. Reasons for endorsing one procedure rather than another lie instead in the extent to which such a procedure satisfies the property of justice, as qualified by a procedural normative criterion. So, for example, the choice between different legal proceedings will depend (also) on the extent to which the alternatives available approximate the criterion in which justice is thought to reside: say, for example, the ideal of equal respect for a person's dignity which would prevent, for instance, personal information regarding the private habits of the defendant being revealed if not directly relevant to the crime of which she is charged.[10] The demands of the principle of equal respect for a person's dignity seem to exceed any reduction to an entitlement theory of the kind Nelson suggests in his attack on pure proceduralism. On this respect-based understanding, justice (as distinct from legitimacy) would require more than establishing who is entitled to be heard – as Hampshire suggested. It would concern also such issues as what kinds of information are relevant, how they can be obtained and disclosed. Such issues certainly exceed reference to entitlements and do not give away any outcome-related commitment.

An outcome theorist could come back to my argument by saying that it is unsound to deny that the value of procedures depends on the value of the outcomes they produce; after all – the outcome theorist would continue – you do not hear many people complaining about the way in which they are treated by procedures when they obtain what they want (Kaplow 1994). This might be sociologically accurate, but since when do philosophers take actual complaints (or the lack thereof) to be a normatively relevant indication of what is (un)just? What this counterargument shows is that, on balance, most people tend *de facto* to give priority to favourable outcomes over unfavourable procedures. It may also succeed in showing that the reason why one is motivated to take part in a procedure has to do with its expected outcome: I wish to participate as participation increases my chances of obtaining a valuable outcome. But this does not show that the standard according to which I will evaluate the moral acceptability of the procedure has exclusively to do with its efficiency in delivering the outcome. In so arguing, I do not wish to deny that the inherent qualities of outcomes count; nor do I wish to argue that the justice of outcomes is always subordinated to that of procedures. But I am committed to claiming that the inherent qualities of procedures matter as they are more or less morally acceptable to persons in their own right. If, for example, we think that justice in politics has to do with treating persons with equal respect, as they are all bearers of the same dignity, then we must agree with David Miller that it is unjust to deal with them through procedures that do not 'give equal attention to [their] claims, [… that do not] attempt to gain an accurate picture of their circumstances [… and that do not] explain the reasons for decision' (Miller 1999, p. 96). And this is the case quite apart from the outcomes procedures of this kind would produce.

Another critical voice could make itself heard at this stage: Richard Arneson's. Despite being mainly targeted at democratic procedures, Arneson's discussion of proceduralism becomes relevant for my present purposes when he addresses legal procedural rights enjoyed by defendants and implied by the principle of due process: 'the right to confront one's accusers, the right to a speedy trial, the right against self-incrimination, the right to counsel, the right to a jury of one's peers, and so on'. Arneson is persuaded that 'this panoply of rights would dissolve if it were discovered that abrogating them wholesale would produce trial verdicts that are fairer (and generate no morally undesirable outcomes of such magnitude as to outweigh the increased fairness of trial verdicts') (Arneson 1993, p. 121). A possible proceduralist rejoinder to Arneson's argument would emphasize that we should certainly want to avoid ending up with the claim that, if procedures are inherently morally irrelevant, literally any procedure enhancing the accuracy of criminal trials should be preferred to those inspired by the principle of due process, even if that included torturing the defendant to establish the truth of the facts. Arneson's replies to this proceduralist rejoinder goes as follows:

> The idea that procedures should be chosen in order to attain morally best results does not mean that the immediate consequences of operating the procedures themselves should be excluded from calculation. [...] My position is that there are no special procedural rights determinable by examining our intuitions about inherently fair procedures (supposed to be independent of our convictions about the substantively fair outcomes that procedures work to reach). (Arneson 1993, p. 121)

Arneson succeeds in showing that when we value the qualities of a procedure we might need to take into consideration the impact its implementation has on those who interact through it. But he thinks that such an impact is part and parcel of the outcomes of that procedure. This is where Arneson's line of reasoning and mine part company, for the *impact* of the application of a procedure should not be mistaken for the *outcome* of that procedure. For example, the outcome of a decision-making procedure is the decision made, whereas its impact may be measured in terms of the enhanced sense of self-esteem of those who took part in it. To say that procedures should only be evaluated on the basis of the outcomes they produce implies that the only justice-relevant criteria we have apply to outcomes. To say, instead, that when we evaluate procedures we should consider the impact their application has on people or on society at large, we are holding a distinctive proceduralist view which, albeit spurious, remains faithful to maintaining different sets of criteria to evaluate outcomes (and their impact) and procedures (and their impact).[11] As an example, consider what Charles Beitz termed the idea of 'fairness as equal respect' (Beitz 1989). This idea focuses on procedures' expressive function: the way in which citizens are treated by the procedures through which they interact in society reveals the consideration institutions have of them. In the case of democratic egalitarian procedures or in legal fair procedures, institutions would express their public recognition of the status of citizens as equals (Griffin 2003, pp. 119–120; for a general discussion of the position, see Elster 1997, pp. 19–25).

So procedures might be valued in the light of their inherent qualities (and independently of the specific outcomes they produce) as they realize in themselves justice-relevant values (e.g., equal respect by treating people in a way commensurate to their dignity) or because their application has a positive impact on those who interact through them (e.g., by treating all people as equals they enhance their self-esteem). In the first case, procedures are valued intrinsically; in the second case, we have a spurious form of proceduralism, attributing value to procedures by virtue of the positive social and psychological effects of an interaction structured through them. In all such cases, on whose respective merits I wish to remain agnostic in this article, the moral acceptability of procedures is independent of their outcomes but depends on how they treat those who interact through them. In other words, even on spurious accounts of proceduralism, theorization about justice concerns the qualities of the procedures through which the participants in a scheme of cooperation interact and remains silent regarding the criteria through which the costs and benefits produced by cooperation should be distributed. In this sense, proceduralism presents itself as a promising complement to outcome theories of justice, capable of capturing normatively relevant considerations on how to evaluate social, political and legal arrangements that go beyond the entitlement-related considerations pertaining to the domain of legitimacy.[12]

Conclusions

I have argued that the task of justifying social order to all those who are subjected to it embodies elements of justice and of legitimacy. We should nonetheless avoid subsuming under a single request for justification three quite separate issues: (1) the justification of authority (who is entitled to exercise coercive power?); (2) the justification of the way in which a society is organized (on what terms should citizens interact with each other?); and (3) the justification of the way in which certain advantages are given to some and not to others (how should the costs and benefits of cooperation be distributed to different citizens?). I have argued that whilst issues in (1) concern the legitimacy of a polity, considerations of justice apply to (2) and (3) as they regard the moral acceptability of the social order.

In my view, failure to account for the distinction between issues of legitimacy and issues of justice bears the main responsibility for political philosophers' neglect of procedures as a proper *locus* of justice. Building on this idea, it has been my concern in this article to explore the sense in which procedures can be viewed as providing a domain for justice-relevant considerations, beyond issues of legitimacy. My main claim has been that in evaluating the justice of a polity, one should not only look at how the costs and benefits of cooperation are distributed but how the cooperation is itself articulated, whether its constitutive procedures treat the co-operators in ways they find morally acceptable. So, for example, the legal system should grant all citizens due process (on procedural grounds) as well as striving to realize just outcomes in the way in which punishments are provided for criminals.

Proceduralism can say something relevant about justice if conceived in these terms, provided that criteria qualifying just procedures are kept separate from those which qualify just outcomes. From this it follows that if the terms of social cooperation are morally acceptable to the parties, this does not mean that its outcomes would likewise be so. In this sense, the account of proceduralism whose relevance in terms of justice I have defended is different from the pure interpretation of proceduralism which can be found in the theories of Rawls and Hampshire and which lies at the heart of proceduralist democratic accounts of legitimacy. In other words, to paraphrase John Elster (Elster 1989, p. 121), the main thrust of my argument does not risk suggesting that the cart of procedural justice be put before the horse of outcome justice. It rather urges that we do not offload the appropriate criteria for what make a good horse onto those which make a good cart.

Acknowledgements

A previous version of this paper was presented at the Central European University Philosophy Seminar. I wish to thank all participants, and especially Gábor Betegh, Ferenc Huoranszki and David Weberman, for helpful discussions. I am also grateful to Andrea Fracasso, Valeria Ottonelli, Enzo Rossi and Federico Zuolo for written comments.

Notes

1. A similar concern is expressed by Nelson (1980, p. 503) and Ehrenberg (2003, p. 168).
2. A formal account of procedural justice is standardly what legal theorists have in mind when making use of this idea. See, for example, Kramer (1997), where procedural (formal) justice is defined as 'concerned only with giving everyone his or her due (as defined by the substance of applicable laws)' (p. 573).
3. For a critical discussion of the sense in which Hampshire's proceduralism may be viewed as inspiring considerations of justice in the management (as distinct from the resolution) of value conflicts in politics, see Ceva (2012).
4. For different conceptions of legitimacy appealing to this concept, see Copp (1999), Beetham (1991), Buchanan (2001) and Simmons (1999).
5. In this paper, I will only explore the tenability of a conceptual separation between the domain of justice and that of legitimacy, but will not take issue with the question of their normative relation (can the scope of justice be defined independently of an account of legitimacy?). Considerations on this point may be found in Enzo Rossi's article in this issue.
6. Outcome theories of legitimacy include a wide range of positions spanning from Hobbes ([1668] 1994) to Raz (1986) (see also Wall 2007).
7. For a discussion, see Glen Newey's article in this issue.
8. For a reading of criminal justice as a scheme of cooperation to which procedural considerations apply, see Morss (2004, p. 646).

9. Needless to say, different conceptions of justice endorse different acceptability tests.
10. Miller uses this idea in a social justice-relevant scenario as follows: 'In cases involving the assignment of benefits, indignity is likely to take the form of requiring people to divulge information about themselves that is normally kept private in order to obtain the benefit. If, for instance, a social security system makes special payments to single parents that are not made to cohabiting couples, this may involve inquiring in people's personal circumstances and checking up on them in a way that is offensive to their dignity' (Miller 1999, p. 101). For a discussion, see Solum (2004) and Marshaw (1985, pp. 158–233).
11. I owe the formulation of spurious proceduralism to a discussion with Valeria Ottonelli.
12. A necessary component of any conception of justice taking into consideration both procedural and outcome-related criteria is a rule of priority to establish how – on specific issues – conflicts between the two sets of criteria are to be addressed should they clash with each other. As I am presently committed to discussing the concept of procedural justice, rather than specific conceptions, I shall limit myself to signalling this important point but leaving it open to further developments elsewhere.

References

Arneson, R. J., 1993. Democratic rights at national and workplace levels. *In*: D. Copp, J. Hampton, and J. E. Roemer, eds. *The idea of democracy*. Cambridge: Cambridge University Press, 118–148.

Beetham, D., 1991. *The legitimation of power*. London: Macmillan.

Beitz, C., 1989. *Political equality*. Princeton, NJ: Princeton University Press.

Buchanan, A., 2001. Political legitimacy and democracy. *Ethics*, 112, 689–719.

Ceva, E., 2007. Plural values and heterogeneous situations. Considerations on the scope for a political theory of justice. *European Journal of Political Theory*, 6, 359–375.

Ceva, E., 2009. Just procedures with controversial outcomes. On the grounds for substantive disputation within a procedural theory of justice. *Res Publica*, 15 (3), 219–235.

Ceva, E., Forthcoming 2012. Just interactions in value conflicts. The adversary argumentation principle. *Politics, Philosophy and Economics*. Doi: 10.1177/1470594x11416780.

Christiano, T., 1996. *The rule of the many*. Boulder, CO: Westview.

Cohen, J., 1994. Pluralism and proceduralism. *Chicago–Kent Law Review*, 69 (3), 589–618.

Copp, D., 1999. The idea of a legitimate state. *Philosophy and Public Affairs*, 28 (1), 3–45.

Dahl, R. A., 1956. *A preface to democratic theory*. Chicago, IL: Chicago University Press.
Ehrenberg, K. M., 2003. Procedural justice and information in conflict-resolving institutions. *Albany Law Review*, 67, 167–209.
Elster, J., 1989. *Solomonic judgements*. Cambridge: Cambridge University Press.
Elster, J., 1997. The market and the forum: three varieties of political theory. *In*: J. Bohman and W. Rehg, eds. *Deliberative democracy*. Cambridge, MA: The MIT Press, 3–24.
Estlund, D., 2007. *Democratic authority*. Princeton, NJ: Princeton University Press.
Griffin, C. G., 2003. Democracy as a non-instrumentally just procedure. *Journal of Political Philosophy*, 11 (1), 111–121.
Hampshire, S., 1999. *Justice is conflict*. London: Duckworth.
Hinsch, W., 2010. Justice, legitimacy, and constitutional rights. *Critical Review of International Social and Political Philosophy*, 13 (1), 39–54.
Hobbes, T., [1668] 1994. *Leviathan*. Indianapolis, IN: Hackett.
Kaplow, L., 1994. The value of accuracy in adjudication: an economic analysis. *Journal of Legal Studies*, 23 (1), 307–401.
Kramer, M. A., 1997. Justice as constancy. *Law and Philosophy*, 16 (6), 561–580.
Locke, J., [1690] 1990. *Second treatise on civil government*. Indianapolis, IN: Hackett.
Marshaw, J. L., 1985. *Due process in the administrative state*. New Haven, CT: Yale University Press.
Miller, D., 1999. *Principles of social justice*. Cambridge, MA: Harvard University Press.
Morss, J. R., 2004. Crime stories: Posnerian pragmatism, Rawlsian pure procedural justice, and the fictional problem. *Deakin Law Review*, 9 (2), 643–654.
Nelson, W., 1980. The very idea of pure procedural justice. *Ethics*, 90 (4), 502–511.
Nussbaum, M., 2006. *Frontiers of justice*. Cambridge, MA: Harvard University Press.
Peter, F., 2008. *Democratic legitimacy*. New York, NY: Routledge.
Rawls, J., 1971. *A theory of justice*. Oxford: Oxford University Press.
Rawls, J., 1993. *Political liberalism*. New York, NY: Columbia University Press.
Raz, J., 1986. *The morality of freedom*. Oxford: Oxford University Press.
Resnick, D., 1977. Due process and procedural justice. *In*: J. R. Pennock and J. W. Chapman, eds. *Due process, Nomos* XVIII. New York, NY: New York University Press, 206–228.
Sadurski, W., 1984. Social justice and legal justice. *Law and Philosophy*, 3 (3), 329–354.
Simmons, J., 1999. Justification and legitimacy. *Ethics*, 109, 739–771.
Solum, L. B., 2004. Procedural justice. *Southern California Law Review*, 78, 181–322.
Waldron, J., 1999. *Law and disagreement*. Oxford: Oxford University Press.
Wall, S., 2007. Democracy and equality. *Philosophical Quarterly*, 57 (228), 416–438.

Equal respect, equal competence and democratic legitimacy

Valeria Ottonelli

Department of Philosophy, University of Genoa, Genoa, Italy

Equal respect for persons is often appealed to as the grounding principle of democratic rule. I argue here that if it needs to account for the specific content of democratic political rights, it must be understood as respect for people as competent political decision-makers. However, the claim that respect is due to people as a response to their *actual* equal competence leads to a conflation of democratic legitimacy and substantive justice, resting on implausible factual assumptions and making it impossible to advocate the effective equalization of political capabilities. Therefore, I suggest that the principle of equal respect should be decoupled from such a claim and be rephrased as simply prescribing that people be *treated* or *publicly recognized* as equally competent. I defend this interpretation against the *publicity objection*, according to which this take on the principle implies insincerity and therefore cannot serve as a public justification for democratic authority.

Introduction

Democratic rule bears a special claim to legitimacy that autocratic or oligarchic institutions lack. It is often argued that what justifies democracy's special claims to legitimacy is that democracy, contrary to autocratic and oligarchic regimes, makes decisions through a process that instantiates the principle of *equal respect* for the members of the political community (for example, Rawls 1996, pp. 319ff., Gutmann and Thompson 2004, pp. 27–49, Marmor 2005, Christiano 2004, Brighouse 1996, Brettschneider 2007, Sadurski 2008).

The reach of the principle of equal respect as the foundation of democratic rule goes beyond the mere justification of popular government: it ensures not only that sovereignty ultimately belongs to the people as a collective entity, but also that political decisions are considered legitimate only insofar as all adult citizens are entitled to participate in making them on an equal footing. This is the principle behind the equal distribution of political rights, which is at the core of our idea of democracy as the government of equals.

In what follows, I will raise a concern about the use of the argument from equal respect as a foundation of democratic legitimacy. As I will argue, if equal respect needs to ground the equal political rights that are distinctive of democracy, it must be conceived of as respect for citizens as equally competent decision-makers in the realm of politics. However, the assumption that people *are* equally competent as political decision-makers, as I will show, not only is implausible, but also bears unwelcome normative implications by conflating legitimacy with justice. Nevertheless, this should not lead us to reject the principle of equal respect as the basis for democratic legitimacy. Rather, I will argue that the principle should be rephrased as stating that citizens must be *treated* with equal respect as equally competent decision-makers, no matter what their actual skills or competence levels. It is this performative sense of respect, I will suggest, that best characterizes democracy as a respectful form of government.

In the next section of this paper I show that equal respect as the foundation of democratic rule is essentially connected to treating people as equally competent decision-makers. In the third section, I argue that the assumption that citizens actually are equally competent decision-makers has unacceptable implications; more specifically, it leads to conflating democratic legitimacy and justice, is indefensible on empirical grounds and prevents one from advocating the effective equalization of political capabilities. In the fourth section, I consider a *minimalist* account of equal respect for people's political competence, which grounds a presumption of equal political competence on the absence of shared standards of justice as a basic fact about politics, and I show that it does not represent a satisfactory solution to these problems. In the fifth section, I argue that claiming that people should be treated as equally competent decision-makers does not necessarily imply believing that they are actually so and I explain how separating the two claims resolves the problems discussed in the third section. In the sixth section, in response to what I call the *publicity objection*, I argue that this interpretation of the principle of equal respect can withstand public scrutiny and can be rationally endorsed by all citizens in a democratic polity.

Equal respect and equal political competence

What is the connection between equally respecting people and recognizing their equal right to rule? The best way to see where the connection lies is by looking at the history of disenfranchised minorities excluded from suffrage until not long ago, like women or dependent workers. These exclusions from full citizenship did not necessarily imply treating the people involved as less than human, or not worthy of equal consideration, like it is the case with other kinds of disrespectful treatment.[1] Rather, the specific kind of disrespect implied in these historical examples consisted in the idea that the members of the disenfranchised groups were not reliable as rulers, due to their material, social and personal situations, which made them incapable of exercising political judgement with sufficient independence and wisdom. Conversely, the equal respect for people that is instantiated by fully democratic decision procedures is respect for them as decision-makers in the political realm and is essentially linked to the recognition of their capacity to participate competently – and with *equal* competence – in decisions of collective relevance.

Democratic government does not simply recognize and value each citizen's competence, but it shows *respect* for it: it does not merely make an instrumental use of the political skills equally owned by citizens, but it publicly expresses deference for the unique contribution that each and every citizen can give to the decision-making process. The institutional form through which this respect is expressed is the entrenchment of equal political rights.

Democratic political rights include the equal right to vote, but also those freedoms that are traditionally seen as essential preconditions of full political participation, such as freedom of association, assembly, speech and press, and the right to go on a strike. These rights protect, make possible and recognize three interrelated forms of political agency and competence: firstly, they recognize that each citizen is capable to discern and voice at best her own needs, interests and values, and to defend them in the first person; secondly, by letting citizens decide not only on personal matters, but also on issues affecting the polity at large, democratic rights recognize that they are capable of the reasonableness and enlarged forms of reasoning required to take into account other people's needs, interests and values as the basis of their judgements about what policies should be adopted; thirdly, and very importantly, by granting not only an equal vote, but also the equal protections required to form political associations and parties, go on a strike and engage in other forms of mobilization and protest, these rights recognize that citizens can be capable of the kind of political wisdom that needs to be exercised when participating in active politics. This level of political competence concerns, for example, the choice of when and how to press an issue for consideration in the political agenda, when it is time actively to mobilize and when to remain silent, which parties to join or support, and which compromises and voting strategies are needed to steer the political process for the best.

Although very sketchy, this brief recollection of the content of democratic rights can help us see that the link between equal respect as respect for equal political competence and the equal right to participate in political decisions is not a contingent historical fact, but reflects an important conceptual truth. This is because equal political competence defines the content or object of equal respect as the ground for equal political rights: unless we specify that equal respect is due to citizens in their capacity *as political actors* in the senses specified, rather than in other capacities, the idea that people should be equally respected is insufficient to explain why we should give them equal political rights, and why political rights should have the specific shape that they do in democratic societies.

To substantiate this claim, I consider here three interpretations of the role of equal respect in justifying democratic rule that do not directly relate equal respect to the recognition of equal political competence. By looking at these examples, we should begin to see that if we ignore that link we fail to account for the role of equal respect in grounding democracy as a distinctive method of government.

According to the first line of argument, democracy is a respectful mode of government because it best guarantees that the fundamental interests and rights of citizens will be respected.[2] Here any reference to political competence is avoided because the stress is on respect not for citizens as decision-makers but as beneficiaries of the decisions to be made in the political arena. The problem with this argument is that it does not highlight what is distinctively and essentially respectful about democracy as opposed to other political regimes. In principle, forms of government other than democracy could fulfil this substantive standard of legitimacy. It might be replied that whatever might be true in principle, as a matter of fact democracy has proven to be the best available way to protect and respect people's fundamental interests. However, even if this empirical claim were granted, this would make democracy only contingently respectful, and in a shallow sense. Saying that democracy is a respectful mode of government because it happens to be the best means to respect people's rights would be like saying that Joan's car is a Thomas-friendly device because it happens to be the only available means of transporting Thomas to the train station this afternoon; it is Joan's intentions that are friendly, not the means through which she furthers them, even if they happen to be the best or only means available. This is to say that there is nothing *essentially* respectful about democracy, as long as it is considered only instrumentally, and this fails to account for the fundamental intuition that democracy itself as a method for making decisions, rather than the ends we want to further by it, is respectful towards people. The reason why we tend not to see this when presented with this kind of outcome-oriented arguments from equal respect is that we usually overlook the fact that they assume, along with the goal of protecting people's interests and rights, that citizens should be let define and protect them *in the first person*. However, this involves recognizing citizens as competent political agents, and valuing democracy because it recognizes and respects this capacity.[3]

The second interpretation takes a different route, explicitly embracing an account of democratic legitimacy focused on the respect due to citizens as decision-makers rather than as mere recipients of the decisions to be made. According to this interpretation, the foundation of democratic rule is the respect we owe to people's natural equal authority in the political domain – conceived of as a basic fact of the state of nature, or deriving from a more fundamental individual right to self-legislation. Since no natural political authority exists among human beings – the argument goes – when the need to make decisions of collective relevance arises, each person is equally entitled to participate in the decision-making process. Apparently, this argument does not relate equal respect to equal political competence, because it treats equal political authority as a basic fact of natural law deriving from the absence of a right to rule over others. However, for this very reason, it fails to explain how people come to have the right to rule over others through majoritarian or other democratic procedures. The mere absence of a natural political authority justifies anarchy, not democracy. Democracy is a form of collective rule, rather than the instantiation of an individual veto power over other people's decisions on one's actions. Thus, the mere argument from the absence of a natural political authority, or from a right to self-legislation, is not enough to account for the legitimacy of democracy.[4] What is needed is an explanation of why every person should have an equal right to rule over others, and here is where the assumption that people should be equally respected as equally competent to act as rulers proves essential in carrying through the argument for democracy.[5]

Finally, consider the discursive justification of democracy grounded on the respect each person is due as participant in a dialogue in which the conditions of social coexistence and cooperation must be justified to everyone. Here equal respect is interpreted as the respect equally owed to each member of the community as a moral agent, to whom the fundamental justification of political institutions is due. According to this interpretation, equal respect is not something owed to people as the result of our recognition of their political competence. Rather, it is a deeper attitude that we adopt every time we enter into discursive interactions with those who share our social space.[6]

For us to recognize that something is missing in this account of equal respect as the foundation of democratic legitimacy it will be sufficient to point out that the equal respect as associated with this discursive foundation of morality is a principle that lies at too deep a level for it to work as a direct justification of democracy. Democracy is not simply the institutionalization of moral interactions grounded in mutual accountability. Instead, it is a complex and public decision procedure that belongs to the political and institutional realm and involves skills and activities that are not reducible to those required by moral agency. As such, it needs to be justified to each member of the political community on the ground of its own distinctive merits as a method of decision. What is distinctive about democracy, contrary to other methods of making decisions of collective relevance, is that it treats all adult members of the political community as equally competent to participate, and it makes this stance public and entrenched by granting all citizens equal political rights. *These* are the distinctive features of democracy that need to be justified to all those affected, and this justificatory work cannot be performed by the basic principle that simply acknowledges a duty to account to each and every citizen for the features of the institutional system; at this point a *different* principle of equal respect, focusing on citizens as political actors, must enter into the argument for democracy.[7]

The conclusion to draw from these illustrations is that the principle of equal respect can work at different levels of the justification for democratic institutions; still, if it needs to work as a justification for what is distinctive about democratic legitimacy – i.e. equality in the distribution of political power – it needs to apply directly to the point in the justification at which equal political rights are established, i.e. it must concern citizens as competent decision-makers in the political realm.

On the demandigness of the recognition of equal competence

It is at this point that a serious difficulty emerges for those who want to found democratic legitimacy on equal respect. As we just saw, if equal respect needs to function as a justification for democratic legitimacy and equal political rights, it must be tied to the recognition of citizens as equally competent decision-makers in the realm of politics. However, the assumption that citizens actually *are* equally competent, and that this (via the principle of equal respect we owe to their equal competence) is the ultimate justification for democratic rule, is highly implausible and bears very unwelcome consequences. Let us consider these claims more closely.

One main source of discomfort is that this way of justifying democratic legitimacy seems to imply that democratic decisions are at least presumptively competent or good. This simply follows once we consider that democratic decisions are made up by the interaction and aggregation of individual contributions to a collective decision process. If people's title to participate ultimately rests on the respect we owe to their competence as decision-makers, then it must be assumed that their participation adds to the decision process in terms of competence, by making its decisions competent or good.

Note that this does not make the argument for democratic legitimacy as grounded on equal respect instrumental or outcome-oriented; we might still argue that the source of the duty to obey democratic authority, in the argument from equal respect, is not the outcome-oriented goal of achieving good or correct decisions, but is rather the procedural principle that mandates to respect each citizen's political competence. Still, the argument needs to imply that individual competence translates into collective competence, and therefore that democracy is a competent method for making decisions. This raises serious and legitimate worries.

First of all, though this account of democratic legitimacy is not instrumental in spirit, it still makes the acceptability of democratic institutions dangerously contingent on democracy's actually being a good decision-making method according to substantive (i.e. outcome oriented) standards of justice, whatever they may be. This means that whenever democracy fails to be a reliable method for making decisions according to those standards, we will have reason to doubt of the very basis of its claim to legitimacy.

Secondly, this account of democratic legitimacy, associated as it is with the presumption that democratic decisions are competent and reliable trackers of correct outcomes in terms of substantive political justice, essentially conflates democratic legitimacy and substantive justice. This implies an account of democratic legitimacy – and of citizens' reasons for obeying democratic decisions – that is simultaneously too demanding and too shallow. According to this account, for respect to be the reason why citizens obey democratic laws, they must also believe that their democratic institutions are an efficient and reliable method of making decisions. This is a very demanding requirement – and one that makes respect somehow inessential as a reason for obeying democratic decisions, because the belief that democracy provides a competent and reliable decision-making procedure might itself serve as a sufficient reason for doing so.

In point of fact, however, we should be concerned even before we look at these implications of the idea that people should be respected as equally competent decision-makers. Indeed, upon closer scrutiny, we should realize that the assumption of equal political competence itself cannot be taken seriously. Consider, for example, those among our fellow citizens who consistently and dogmatically hold racist, sexist or wildly utopian views; it is very difficult to believe that are just about as competent as anybody else at making decisions of collective relevance. And even if we did not know from our direct experience that many of our fellow citizens entertain stupid or insane political views, we could conjecture it from our general knowledge of human nature and of those conditions that can gravely impair our capacity to reason and judge. We are all too aware of the differences in cultural background and in opportunities to access correct and exhaustive information – and of the psychological and social effects of domination, oppression and class, gender and race biases – to be seriously confident in the fact that people are equally well positioned and equally likely to be competent political decision-makers.[8] Thus, we would still have reason to reject a blanket judgement regarding the equal distribution of political wisdom among our fellow citizens.

The assumption that people are equally competent at making political judgements is not only difficult to adhere to but also leads to dangerous practical consequences. Such an assumption requires that we ignore and forget all those conditions that actually impair people's capacity for correct political judgement. This is a serious problem in so far as many of these factors could be and must be redressed, thus enabling people to exercise their political powers effectively and competently. The list of these factors is in principle very long,[9] but let me mention here three of them. First of all, people tend to be unequally competent as political decision-makers because of the existing asymmetry in their capacity to collect and process information, which in most democratic societies is due to the failures and biases of the media and educational systems. Another obvious cause of unequal competence that needs to be redressed is the cultural subalternity of oppressed minorities, who may be manipulated by dominant groups and remain unable to develop an independent perspective on their social world. The third condition that negatively affects equal political competence is the asymmetrical distribution of organizational resources, i.e. what John Stuart Mill used to call the 'power of combination' (Mill 1977a, p. 163). Being part of a network of political and social relationships is an essential element of the capacity to form correct and mature judgements about politics, and many subordinated groups, like recent immigrants and (in many countries) women, still significantly lack such power. On the other hand, there are also people who run the risk of being trapped within cultural and political enclaves that prevent them from accessing the full range of data and perspectives available in the public sphere; they are part of a network, but one that has distortive effects on their capacity to assess facts and policies.[10] All these conditions can and should be addressed through the mobilization of economic, cultural and political resources. But to do so we first need to recognize the existence of such factors and analyse their causes and effects. This is made impossible by a blanket denial of the inequality in people's capacity to make competent political judgements and exercise all the other political skills that are called for in collective decision-making.

The minimalist approach to equal respect

It might be objected that we are assuming here too thick a notion of political competence, and that this is the source of all our problems. What is being assumed is that people are equally competent according to some shared standards of what counts as a good or well-made decision, and what counts as political skills, whereas it could be argued that equal respect for people as political decision-makers does not imply anything of the sort. The claim that citizens are equally competent does not need to be grounded in a substantive theory of correct political judgement but could be based instead on the *absence* of such a theory, i.e. on the acknowledgement that we deeply disagree not only about what the correct decisions are but also about what kind of reasoning is more apt to lead to them.[11]

It is along these lines that Jeremy Waldron has argued for what might be called a 'minimalist' account of the equal respect that is distinctive of democracy: our duty to respect our fellow citizens as decision-makers simply derives from the recognition of reasonable and rational disagreement as the result of the *burdens of judgement*: when we are facing disagreement about justice, in order to explain why people's views diverge we should not resort to the assumption that some of them must be ignorant, biased, or wicked. On the contrary, the explanation must be sought in the fact that 'there are a number of distinct intelligences, and … it is not unexpected, not unnatural, not irrational to think that reasonable people would differ' (Waldron 1999b, p. 112). Giving each citizen an equal voice is but a way to acknowledge that disagreement is legitimate and therefore nobody can claim superior authority on political justice.

Once we have assumed such an agnostic standard for assessing equal competence, the recognition of people's equal capacity to make decisions will stop at the individual level and will not translate into competence at the collective level. Majority rule and the 'one person, one vote' principle will then be simply understood as *fair* devices for making decisions, i.e. procedures that ensure that every citizen has an equal chance to see her view prevail – in due recognition of the respect owed to each citizen's judgment as equally likely to be correct.

This minimalist account might look as a promising strategy for avoiding the problems raised by a fuller conception of equal respect. However, it should be noted that it comes at a heavy cost: it leaves us with a very impoverished idea of what equal democratic participation entails, and a very impoverished notion of the equal respect that is embodied in democratic institutions. Let me expand briefly on both points.

The minimalist approach is by its very nature and purpose incompatible with taking into account the *aggregative* dimension of democratic procedures, i.e. the fact that in the democratic method as we know it the individual contributions to the final decisions are *combined*, rather than *selected*. As it has been pointed out by some critics (Estlund 2008, p. 95, Marmor 2002), because of this downplaying of the aggregative dimension of democracy the minimalist approach, in fact, cannot even account for one of its defining features, i.e. majority rule: the mere principle of fairness as equal opportunity to see one's views prevail does not require majority rule, but would be satisfied by a lottery-like device or any random procedure for selecting one of the views among those expressed by citizens.[12] What is even more important in this context, is that if this minimalist account needs to work as a public justification for democratic government, citizens themselves must understand what they are doing when they participate in democratic politics as simply expressing their own reasoned views about what is right, then leaving to some external and possibly random mechanism to decide which one will prevail. But this seems to be a very poor account of the kind of agency that is implied by democratic politics and of the political competence that is recognized to citizens by the whole range of political liberties. Although these are individual rights and the equal respect they signify and embody is respect for individual persons, the agency they protect and make possible is the participation in a *collective* decision-making process in which each one employs their powers in order to steer the final result towards the best outcome, taking direct responsibility in guiding the process of accommodation and mediation of the different political views. This means that the minimalist account downplays, along with the collective and aggregative dimensions of democratic decision-making, also the complex forms of reasonableness and political wisdom that are associated with the understanding of democracy as a collective process of decision-making. The cost for adopting a minimalist account of equal respect as a foundation of democracy, thus, is not only a poor account of what democracy implies, but also a mortifying impoverishment of the very notion of equal respect involved.

What is even worse is that such a strategy does not really solve the problems associated with the maximalist conception of equal respect. Even as an agnostic and minimalist statement about the impossibility of establishing levels of individual competence – as opposed to establishing equal competence according to shared standards of justice – the claim that all citizens should be considered as equally competent is patently unsound. Waldron's appeal to the doctrine of the burdens of judgement is misplaced in this context. This doctrine was devised to explain how disagreement is *possible* even when people are rational and reasonable (Rawls 1996, pp. 55ff.); it was not meant to prove that *all* disagreement is rational and reasonable. As a matter of fact, although there is much genuine reasonable disagreement, and we cannot harshly disqualify as incompetent any view we do not agree with, this should not lead us to assume that all political views must be considered rational, reasonable or wise; in many cases we do not only have good reasons for not considering them so, but also possess reliable explanations about how such views can develop out of ignorance, ill-faith, ideology and other failures of political competence.

Secondly, the minimalist interpretation does not offer a better account of the role of equal respect in justifying democratic legitimacy than does a maximalist account. The minimalist interpretation ultimately grounds the argument for democracy in an agnostic attitude about what substantive justice requires: if citizens are due equal respect as political actors – and therefore equal political rights – because each one is equally likely to be right about justice, then our respect for people's equal competence must be associated with the belief that what justice requires is ultimately underdetermined and unknowable. Also in the minimalist account, then, like in the maximalist we have considered earlier, the argument for democratic legitimacy grounded on equal respect stands or falls with an account of what substantive justice requires. Here again we lose track of the intuition that we have a reason for obeying democratic decisions which is independent of our convictions about what substantive justice requires and how to establish it at best.[13]

Equal respect as equally respectful treatment

All these issues stem from the fact that both the minimalist and the maximalist accounts examined so far are tied to the assumption that the equal respect due to people as participants in democratic decisions is due to them as an acknowledgement of their *actual* skills and virtues as responsible and competent decision-makers. The minimalist account, indeed, attempts to dilute this assumption by phrasing it as a negative presumption deriving from the absence of shared standards of correct political judgement. As we have seen, however, this approach makes for a poor account of democratic political agency, and in any case, even under this purely negative and minimalist guise, the presumption of equal competence is still very hard to accept.

I suggest that, if we want to overcome these problems, we must disentangle the idea that equal respect can serve as a principle of democracy from any factual assumptions about citizens' equal competence. This entails shifting the phrasing of the principle. Equal respect should be interpreted as a requirement of respectful *treatment*, rather than as a requirement of sincere responsiveness to competence. In other words, equal respect should be conceived of not as a reflection of the actual recognition of people's equal competence but instead as the requirement that people be treated *as if* they were equally competent – independently of the actual evidence about their skills – by giving them an equal opportunity to participate in the formation of collective decisions through the enjoyment of equal voting rights and the overall scheme of equal political liberties.

The question remains of what might be the rationale for the duty to respect people as equally competent political agents, if it is not the belief that they are indeed equally competent. I suggest that this rationale could be found in the performative function served by treating citizens with respect as political actors. Representing each citizen as equally worthy of respect as a political actor is a fundamental goal in democratic societies because political power has traditionally been one of the most visible and entrenched sites of the hierarchical organization and self-representation of society along gender, race and class lines. If we understand the democratic ideal as the ideal of a society in which people treat each other as equals,[14] and in which entrenched social hierarchies are publicly disavowed, then treating people as equally worthy of respect as rulers is an important part of the project. According to this notion, procedural equality in the realm of lawmaking is an independent and self-standing political ideal, along with substantive fairness or economic efficiency,[15] which regulates the interactions between citizens according to the fundamental egalitarian goal that all hierarchies of status entrenched in political institutions (and their attached justifications) should be abolished. Indeed, for the sake of this egalitarian goal, we might be willing to pay the cost of undergoing the consequences of sub-optimal decisions in terms of substantive justice or efficiency. This can happen because the level of competence of the people deciding is less than optimal, or because the decision procedures needed to represent people as equally worthy of respect as decision-makers are less efficient than more autocratic methods. Still, we might prefer to use procedures that treat people with equal respect as decision-makers in order to fulfil the ideal of a society in which people treat and *represent* each other as equals.

Disentangling equal respect in the political realm from positive assessments of people's competence allows us to overcome the objections to both the maximalist and the minimalist accounts of the principle of equal respect that we have explored so far. First of all, the principle can be articulated as requiring that we respect people as political decision-makers according to the full understanding of competence implied by the maximalist conception. This includes the complex forms of political interaction and wisdom associated with the understanding of political rights as rights to participate in a collective decision-making process. At the same time, because the principle simply requires treating people *as if* they were equally competent in this fullest sense and is explicitly disentangled from any assumptions about their actual competence, it is not necessarily associated with faith in the epistemic powers of democracy. This makes the principle completely autonomous and separate from any outcome-oriented justification of democracy because the factual conditions on which the two justifications rest are different.

Furthermore, once the principle of equal respect is interpreted as simply requiring respectful treatment and is disentangled from factual assumptions about people's actual capacities, it obviously does not require us to form overly optimistic beliefs about the political competence of our fellow citizens. This approach to the justification of democracy allows us to entertain a more realistic account of the real sources of disagreement and conflict within existing democracies, which lead people to have different views not only because they have different interests and perspectives, or because their use of reason has led them in different directions, but also because they are unequally capable of exercising their rationality, reasonableness and wisdom in the political realm.

In addition, this rendering of the principle is compatible with the acknowledgement of and the intervention against the most obvious causes of political incompetence. The principle of equal respect requires that we treat people as equally competent insofar as the distribution of political liberties and rights is concerned, but it does not preclude the establishment of programmes intended to enhance people's opportunities to develop political competence if they have been disadvantaged in this regard.

Finally, this way of articulating the principle of equal respect offers a better account of democratic legitimacy and of the reasons that citizens may have for obeying democratic decisions. Since it does not rely on epistemic assumptions about the individual and collective capacity to track correct decisions, it does not conflate democratic legitimacy with justice. This means that it can explain how citizens can have a strong reason to obey democratic decisions out of respect for their fellow citizens even when they have little faith in the actual epistemic powers of democracy or are unwilling to admit that the views of their fellow citizens are equally competent. This, in a way, makes the respect-based account of democratic legitimacy less demanding than it would be otherwise. At the same time it accounts for the normative force and value of equal respect as an independent principle of legitimacy, which does not collapse into substantive principles of justice or an agnostic attitude about what justice requires.

The publicity objection

In a sense, the interpretation of the principle of equal respect as equally respectful treatment should appear as the most natural interpretation in the context of a normative theory of democracy. If what we need is a justification for *public* institutions, then the principle appealed to must concern how people should *treat* each other rather than how they should feel or what they should think about each other.

Nevertheless, conceiving of the principle of equal respect as the mere requirement that we treat people with equal respect in their capacity of decision-makers, even though this treatment is not grounded in any sincere belief in their equal competence, may be seen as a kind of hypocrisy or insincere behaviour, which is an inappropriate foundation for democratic rule. This worry can be phrased more precisely, and from a perspective of immediate concern for political philosophy, as the *publicity objection*.

Any principle of democracy, the objection goes, must fulfil the requirement of publicity, i.e. it must be able to be made public and offered to the public at large as a justification for democratic institutions.[16] The principle of equal respectful treatment, though, by requiring us to treat people as equally competent independently of any actual belief about their actual competence (or even despite the belief and evidence that they are incompetent) cannot pass this test. This is because if it were made public, the principle would be self-defeating: once they knew that they might be given respect insincerely, without there being a genuine recognition of their equal political competence, citizens would stop valuing being treated respectfully.

As biting as this objection might appear at first sight, I would nevertheless like to defend the conception of equal respect as equally respectful treatment by pointing to some empirical and normative considerations about equal respect that the objection seems to overlook.

As a preliminary point we should observe that the objection, as phrased here, assumes that the public knowledge of the unequal political competence of the members of the political community must come as a list of specific people called by name and classified as less than fully competent. However, this does not have to be the case even where special programmes are set up for the purpose of redressing unequal political competence. As long as those programmes are not targeted to specific people and they are justified as opportunities and social resources made available to the citizens at large rather than conditions for the enjoyment of political rights, there is no reason to presume that anybody should feel stigmatized as less worthy of respect than others, and therefore unable to enjoy the public recognition of equal competence associated with the equal distribution of political rights. This is clearly the case, for example, with one of the most important institutions traditionally associated with the advancement of equal political competence, i.e. public education.

Secondly, and more importantly, the idea that being treated respectfully is worth nothing if it does not come with sincere respect from others overlooks some important features of respect as a social and political relation. The assumption behind the objection considered is that people seek respectful treatment not for its own sake but because it expresses and reveals sincere deference and esteem by one's peers. However, this is not the case, even when respectful treatment publicly *signifies* esteem and deference. To appreciate this point, consider the phenomenology of theoretical authority when it is institutionalized and embodied in fixed social relations, like those between the elderly and the young or religious authorities and believers. Those who are in authority might like the idea that those who obey them do so because they sincerely feel that they have superior knowledge. However, they do not expect them to exercise that kind of judgement every time they give their advice or issue a command; on the contrary, they expect them to obey irrespectively of what they think. This is part of what being an authority is: it is entrenched social power that conveys hierarchies of status independently of the actual beliefs and feelings of those who obey, provided that the reason why they obey is that they recognize the authority's legitimacy and the social meanings attached to it. By the same token, historically subordinated social groups may want and value being treated with respect as decision-makers, even if they know very well that many people around them may not feel, deep in their hearts, that they are equally competent.

This brings us to a third reason for thinking that the value of the public and institutional recognition of equal competence cannot be undermined by the lack of an actual belief in equal competence: if this were the case, the achievement of equal political competence, in all circumstances in which it is not already established, would be impossible, given that being treated as an equally competent agent is a preliminary condition for becoming one.

Here the most vivid analogy is provided by autonomy, which is a kind of practical competence constituted by various intellectual and practical skills. For those skills to develop, they need to be exercised within the appropriate frame of social rules and legal rights;[17] however, in principle these rights should only be granted to those capable of exercising them, and this creates an obvious vicious circle, since the relevant skills cannot be acquired unless they are exercised. Emancipating people requires breaking this vicious circle by asserting their autonomy and giving them the social and institutional tools to exercise it without previously ascertaining whether they are capable of doing so. I suggest that the same is true of political competence. Treating people with the respect due to competent decision-makers is an essential condition for their being able to develop the required competence, and there is no way to emancipate historically subordinated groups or to bring to full political awareness those who have been blinded by ideology other than that of providing them with equal status as competent decision-makers.

If all this is true, then the lack of an established belief in the equal and fully developed political competence of every citizen need not undermine the public endorsement of the principle that we should treat our fellow citizens with equal respect as political decision-makers. Therefore, the principle passes the publicity test.

Conclusion

I have argued here that *if* equal respect can be a principle of democratic legitimacy at all, then it needs to be interpreted as the principle that citizens must be *treated* with equal respect as competent decision-makers in the political realm, whereas this should not imply that they actually *are* equally competent.

In principle, this argument does not rule out alternative theories of what makes democracy a legitimate form of government, what makes it a reliable way to implement substantive justice, or what justifies equal political rights. What this discussion was meant to challenge, instead, are those accounts of equal respect as the foundation of democratic legitimacy that rely too hastily and confidently on the assumption that citizens actually possess equal political competence. Not only do such accounts rely on patently implausible assumptions, but also they come at the cost of significantly downplaying the meaning and reach of democratic political rights and the role of the very principle of equal respect as the basis for the distinctive legitimacy of democratic institutions.

Acknowledgements

I received very helpful comments on earlier versions of this paper from Enrico Biale, Teresa Britton, Anna Elisabetta Galeotti and the audience at the Pavia 8th

Graduate Conference in Political Philosophy. I am also very grateful to the Editors of this issue, Emanuela Ceva and Enzo Rossi, for their insightful suggestions.

Notes

1. Treating people as unworthy of equal consideration, or less than moral beings, surely was not implied, for example, by the well-known Kantian argument for denying women the right to vote, or by J. S. Mill's reasons for giving manual workers lesser votes than their employers (Kant 1996, p. 92; Mill 1977b, ch. VIII).
2. On the relevance of these outcome-oriented considerations for the justification of democracy, see Dworkin (1987) and Arneson (2004).
3. Consider, for example, Thomas Christiano's argument about democracy being a respectful form of government because it makes the equal concern for each and every citizen public by granting each one equal political rights (Christiano 2004, 2008). The argument would not function properly if we did not assume that people are equally capable of assessing their own interests.
4. This is not to deny that self-legislation is an essential (although not exhaustive) element of the kind of agency recognized and respected by democratic rights.
5. An argument for democracy along these lines is presented by Jeremy Waldron in his account of Locke's 'physics of consent' (Waldron 1999a, pp. 124–166). It is important to note that Waldron is well aware of the fact that the argument from natural equality is incomplete; in fact, he completes it by adding an additional premise about the equality of judgment among human beings that entitles each one to have a say in political decisions. This premise rests on the doctrine of the *burdens of judgement*, which is discussed below.
6. Here the obvious reference is Stephen Darwall's notion of 'recognition respect' (Darwall 1977), which has recently been developed into an openly discursive perspective (Darwall 2006). For an analogous account of equal respect as the foundation of political liberalism, see Larmore (1987, pp. 62–63).
7. It is important to note that in his influential account of equal respect as the foundation of political liberalism Larmore (1987, p. 61) explicitly states that his notion of equal respect would not (and should not) be sufficient to justify strictly egalitarian policies.
8. See the classical and ever-growing literature on voter knowledge and rationality and on civic engagement (for example, Almond and Verba 1963, Delli Carpini and Keeter 1996, Popkin and Dimock 1999, Caplan 2007). These studies tend to reach pessimistic conclusions about the average political competence and – what is more important here – to register *unequal* levels of competence. On the failures of uneducated common sense reasoning, see also Gaus (1996, pp. 130ff.).
9. For two recent analyses, see Verba (2006) and Olson (2006).
10. What I have in mind here are phenomena of 'group polarization' as discussed by Sunstein (2001).
11. Of course, a negative case for equal political competence could also be established by showing that citizens are equally *in*competent at making political decisions, so that nobody can claim superior authority. However, I do not consider this idea here because it would not be an argument based on equal *respect*.

12. Estlund (2008) convincingly argues that Waldron's endorsement of majority rule in fact reveals that he is not loyal to his own claim that mere fairness, rather than some principle of aggregation of individual competence, is the ground for democratic legitimacy.
13. It might be worth specifying that there being a reason for obeying democratic decisions that is independent of their correctness does not imply that such a reason always overrides considerations of substantive justice. The present discussion, however, is not concerned with how to balance these possibly conflicting normative considerations.
14. A paradigmatic statement of such a conception is Elizabeth Anderson's idea of democratic equality (Anderson 1999). In Anderson (2009) this idea takes a perfectionist bent, which I do not endorse here.
15. On this conception of procedural equality, see Young (1990).
16. What I have in mind here especially is Jon Elster's use of Kant's *transcendental formula of public right* in his classical discussion of self-defeating political theories (Elster 1983, pp. 91ff.).
17. On the social conditions for autonomy, see Meyers (1991) and Oshana (2006, pp. 86ff.).

References

Almond, G. A. and Verba, S., 1963. *The civic culture, Political attitudes and democracy in five nations*. London: Sage.

Anderson, E., 1999. What is the point of equality? *Ethics*, 109 (2), 287–337.

Anderson, E., 2009. Democracy: instrumental vs. non-instrumental value. *In*: T. Christiano and J. P. Christman, eds. *Contemporary debates in political philosophy*. Oxford: Blackwell, 213–27.

Arneson, R., 2004. Democracy is not intrinsically just. *In*: K. Dowding, R. E. Goodin, and C. Pateman, eds. *Justice and democracy*. Cambridge: Cambridge University Press, 40–58.

Brettschneider, C., 2007. *Democratic rights*. Princeton, NJ: Princeton University Press.

Brighouse, H., 1996. Egalitarianism and equal availability of political influence. *Journal of Political Philosophy*, 4 (2), 118–141.

Caplan, B., 2007. *The myth of the rational voter*. Princeton, NJ: Princeton University Press.

Christiano, T., 2004. The authority of democracy. *Journal of Political Philosophy*, 12 (3), 266–290.

Christiano, T., 2008. *The constitution of equality*. Oxford: Oxford University Press.

Darwall, S., 1977. Two kinds of respect. *Ethics*, 88 (1), 36–49.

Darwall, S., 2006. *The second-person standpoint*. Cambridge, MA: Harvard University Press.

Delli Carpini, M. X. and Keeter, S., 1996. *What Americans know about politics and why it matters*. New Haven, CT: Yale University Press.
Dworkin, R., 1987. What is equality? Part 4: Political equality. *University of San Francisco Law Review*, 22 (1), 1–30.
Elster, J., 1983. *Sour grapes*. Cambridge: Cambridge University Press.
Estlund, D., 2008. *Democratic authority*. Princeton, NJ: Princeton University Press.
Gaus, G., 1996. *Justificatory liberalism*. Oxford: Oxford University Press.
Gutmann, A. and Thompson, D., 2004. *Why deliberative democracy?*. Princeton, NJ: Princeton University Press.
Kant, I., 1996. *Metaphysics of morals*. Cambridge: Cambridge University Press.
Larmore, C., 1987. *Patterns of moral complexity*. Cambridge: Cambridge University Press.
Marmor, A., 2002. Jeremy Waldron, law and disagreement and the dignity of legislation. *Ethics*, 112 (2), 410–415.
Marmor, A., 2005. Authority, equality and democracy. *Ratio Juris*, 18 (3), 315–345.
Meyers, D. T., 1991. *Self, society and personal choice*. New York, NY: Columbia University Press.
Mill, J. S., 1977a. Tocqueville on democracy in America. *In*: *Collected Works*. Vol. XVIII. Toronto, ON: University of Toronto Press.
Mill, J. S., 1977b. Considerations on representative government. *In*: *Collected Works*. Vol. XIX. Toronto, ON: University of Toronto Press.
Olson, K., 2006. *Reflexive democracy: political equality and the welfare state*. Cambridge, MA: MIT Press.
Oshana, M., 2006. *Personal autonomy in society*. Aldershot: Ashgate.
Popkin, S. M. and Dimock, M. A., 1999. Political knowledge and citizen competence. *In*: S. L. Elkin and K. E. Soltan, eds. *Citizen competence and democratic institutions*. University Park, PA: Pennsylvania State University Press, 117–146.
Rawls, J., 1996. *Political liberalism*. New York, NY: Columbia University Press.
Sadurski, W., 2008. *Equality and legitimacy*. Oxford: Oxford University Press.
Sunstein, C., 2001. *Republic.com*. Princeton, NJ: Princeton University Press.
Verba, S., 2006. Fairness, equality and democracy: three big words. *Social Research*, 72 (2), 499–540.
Waldron, J., 1999a. *The dignity of legislation*. Cambridge: Cambridge University Press.
Waldron, J., 1999b. *Law and disagreement*. Oxford: Oxford University Press.
Young, I. M., 1990. *Justice and the politics of difference*. Princeton, NJ: Princeton University Press.

Democratic legitimacy, legal expressivism, and religious establishment

Simon Căbulea May

Department of Philosophy, Virginia Tech, Blacksburg, VA, USA

I argue that some instances of constitutional religious establishment can be consistent with an expressivist interpretation of democratic legitimacy. Whether official religious endorsements disparage or exclude religious minorities depends on a number of contextual considerations, including the philosophical content of the religion in question, the attitudes of the majority, and the underlying purpose of the official status of the religious doctrine.

Introduction

My aim in this paper is to defend the claim that the constitutional establishment of a majority religion can be consistent with an expressivist interpretation of democratic political legitimacy, even in the familiar circumstances of religious diversity characteristic of a liberal society. I do not claim that religious establishment is generally legitimate; I argue instead that even some purely symbolic affirmations of religion violate the requirements of democratic legitimacy. Nor do I claim that religious establishment is ever morally justified. A principle of secularism may constrain justifiable government action without also being a condition of democratic legitimacy.[1] Even if the state should be neutral in philosophical debates about religious doctrines, legitimate governments are, within broad limits, morally entitled to act in ways that they should not. My contention is that at least some instances of religious establishment can fall within the limits set by the democratic conception of legitimacy.

The paper contains five sections. First, I set out two principles constitutive of the democratic conception. The principle of *equal standing* states that all citizens must be able to participate in political processes on equal terms. The principle of *equal respect* states that governments may only exercise political power in ways that treat citizens as equals. Second, I invoke the expressivist approach to law advanced by Elizabeth Anderson and Richard Pildes (Anderson and Pildes 2000) to argue that the democratic legitimacy of government actions can turn on their expressive social meaning. Third, I discuss two expressivist arguments against official endorsements of religion, as presented by Christopher Eisgruber and Lawrence Sager (Eisgruber and Sager 2007) and by Martha Nussbaum (Nussbaum 2008) in their accounts of the Establishment Clause of the United States Constitution. These arguments state that such endorsements *disparage* adherents of minority religions or *exclude* them from full membership in the polity. Fourth, I set out an account of the expressive meaning of government action that shows why some purely symbolic state affirmations of religion are illegitimate. Fifth, I argue that this account also demonstrates that some constitutional establishments of religion do not express disparagement or exclusion. Consequently, the two arguments do not show that the constitutional establishment of a majority religion in a diverse liberal society is invariably illegitimate. I conclude by way of a brief discussion of the implications of my thesis for Establishment Clause jurisprudence.

Democratic legitimacy

A legitimate government possesses the exclusive moral right to rule a society (Simmons 1999, Copp 1999, Christiano 2008, pp. 241–243). Political power may be legitimately exercised in ways that are unjust, unfair, or otherwise unjustifiable (Rawls 2005, pp. 427–428).[2] Legitimacy concerns the conditions under which a government is morally entitled to make, implement, and enforce its decisions, and not, within broad limits, the moral quality of the decisions it makes. In a democracy, a majority party's right to exercise authority as it proposes follows from its electoral victory and not from the substantive merits of its electoral manifesto. Supporters of opposition parties might criticise the justifiability of a government's policies without impugning their legitimacy. A government may legitimately allow an endangered animal to be hunted, for instance, or impose strict controls on the consumption of substances that should be more freely available. Similarly, although the establishment of an official religion may be unjustified, and perhaps deeply objectionable, it does not follow that it cannot be a legitimate exercise of the right to make political decisions.

Legitimacy involves a deep asymmetry in discretion and deference. It entitles certain people to the authority to make potentially momentous decisions about the exercise of state power, and creates some range of prima facie moral duties on the part of other agents to respect that authority.[3] The group of people elected to the Westminster Parliament claim a moral right – and not just a legal power – that the crowd at Old Trafford and the members of the Aristotelian Society do not have. An important problem for any account of political legitimacy is to explain how this profound inequality can be justified if all citizens have an equal moral status. The democratic conception supposes that the solution to this problem is to demonstrate how political authority can be made consistent with equality: governments acquire the right to rule only when they are elected and govern in accordance with the equal status of all citizens. The two principles provide a fuller specification of this requirement.

The first principle states that all citizens must have equal standing in fundamental political processes. This principle governs the *procedural* genesis of laws rather than their substantive content. Equal standing requires that citizens have an equal vote and an equal right to stand for office, and that the background conditions necessary for the effective use of these rights are in place. These conditions include the familiar rights of free association, speech, and conscience, as well as the social and economic capability to take part in political processes on the same footing as one's peers. Legitimacy does not require an egalitarian distribution of wealth, but it is undermined to the extent that some citizens are simply too impoverished to participate in politics. If citizens did not have equal standing in political processes, then the origin of a government's authority would not be consistent with the equal status of all, and its claim to legitimacy would not be warranted. An undemocratic regime cannot simply appeal to the substantive merits of its policies. Political authority is possessed and exercised by some individuals rather than others, and an account of political legitimacy must explain why it is these specific people who may govern, whether or not their decisions are justifiable (Buchanan 2004, p. 249). The threat to equality is generated by the disparity in political authority itself and not just by what a government might do with that authority. The possession of political power in a manner inconsistent with the equal standing of citizens can sometimes be justified, especially in conditions where only an undemocratic regime can avert an impending catastrophe. But this justification would not demonstrate that such a regime possesses legitimacy, as I have defined the term, since it would not constitute an adequate justification for the inequality in moral rights that legitimacy involves (cf. Buchanan 2004, p. 259). Although citizens may have independent moral reasons to acquiesce in the regime's rule, it would not itself have any moral claim to their allegiance if they did not have an equal say in its acquisition of power. Should the regime be overthrown by equally virtuous and equally competent rebels in a bloodless *coup d'état*, none of its moral rights would be violated and it would have no moral claim to restoration. In contrast, the democratic conception supposes that an elected government has acquired the right not to be deposed by rebels for the duration of its term, and would have a strong claim to restoration if it were.

The second principle states that the government must treat citizens with equal concern and respect in the exercise of its authority. This principle governs the *substantive* content of public policies independently of their procedural genesis. A democratic government has the moral right to impose unjustified policies, but there are limits to this right. For instance, elected representatives are entitled to enact laws that affect property prices, even in unjust ways, but they have no moral right to pass such laws just so that the value of their own personal property increases. These laws may have no deleterious consequences for the equal standing of citizens in political processes, but in acting for that reason the legislators treat themselves as more deserving of the benefits of government than other citizens. Since they fail to respect other citizens as equals, the justification of their authority is incomplete. The challenge of political legitimacy is to show how the right to rule can be consistent with the fundamental equality of all citizens, so it cannot be exercised in a manner that is inconsistent with this value. The genesis of political power in a democratic election is an important element in the justification of a government's right to rule. But those who claim the entitlement to decide political questions must be able to explain to their fellow citizens why their exclusive authority is consistent with the equal status of all. They cannot simply point to the popular origin of their authority as an adequate explanation if they are also prepared to act in ways that belie the value they are required to respect.

Since the democratic conception incorporates a substantive principle, it differs from pure proceduralist theories, which hold that the outcomes of legitimate political processes are legitimate whatever they may be. The conception also differs from substantive theories that draw on a broad set of core values in addition to equality. For instance, John Rawls's (2005) liberal principle of legitimacy incorporates a criterion of reciprocity that rules out constitutional arrangements that are not reasonably acceptable to all.[4] As my present concern is whether the democratic conception *itself* precludes religious establishment, I leave aside whether it is a complete account of political legitimacy. The two principles do not impose as many constraints on government practices as broader substantive theories; Rawls's liberal principle clearly rules out religious establishment in all normal circumstances of religious diversity. Nevertheless, the democratic conception is a demanding theory of legitimacy in its own right.

Legal expressivism

Expressivist theories of law state that government actions should be evaluated in terms of their expression of appropriate attitudes (Anderson and Pildes 2000, p. 1520), particularly attitudes towards people (p. 1509). The law is not simply a causal mechanism. Instead, expressivists believe that the law has an objective social meaning as the purposive action of the state. This expressive meaning is not constituted by the subjective attitudes that citizens have about the law (pp. 1523–1527). For example, some may feel offended by decisions they falsely believe dishonour important values. Determining the expressive meaning of a government action is a *normative* question that turns on how the attitudes it expresses should be understood and interpreted in the light of relevant social facts and applicable norms (p. 1513).

Expressivism identifies two distinct dimensions of moral and legal evaluation. First, it is objectionable in itself for a government to express improper attitudes towards its citizens, irrespective of consequences. Second, the communication of improper attitudes through government action can harm citizens by immediately changing the relationships in which they stand (Anderson and Pildes 2000, pp. 1527–1531). This expressive harm is distinct from the material harms that laws can cause. Social relationships are partly constituted by a shared understanding of their governing attitudes. Two people would not be in a genuine friendship, for instance, if they did not both realise their mutual concern for each other and its role in guiding their common activity. In the public realm, the state possesses the unique authority to define the terms of political relationships. Thus, if the state conveys an improper attitude about citizens, it can constitute them as participants in a noxious relationship.

Expressivists can articulate the democratic conception of legitimacy in a manner that tracks the two dimensions of evaluation. On this approach, the principle of equal respect regulates the attitudes towards citizens that a government may express. Not all improper attitudes are illegitimate, but no government has the right to express unequal concern and respect for citizens. Similarly, the principle of equal standing regulates the kinds of political relationships that may exist. Not all noxious relationships undermine legitimacy, but the government's right to rule requires that no citizens be subordinated in the public realm. Thus, government action with a particular expressive meaning can immediately violate each of the democratic principles, quite apart from its broader causal consequences.

Two sceptical challenges can be raised against any expressivist analysis of political legitimacy. First, there may be no such thing as the objective social meaning of a law or policy. Political decisions are the result of complex processes undertaken by citizens who hold quite different interpretations of the government actions they effect. Expressivism thus needs some criterion of correct interpretation, otherwise there can be no fact of the matter about whether these decisions express illegitimate attitudes. Call this the indeterminacy challenge. Second, even if a public policy does have a determinate expressive meaning, this may be too morally insubstantial a feature to support a charge of illegitimacy. The analysis must explain why legitimacy is sensitive to expressive harms when it is not always sensitive to unjust material harms.

The most powerful example in support of legal expressivism is the treatment of racial segregation in American constitutional jurisprudence. This example helps parry both challenges to the expressivist analysis of democratic legitimacy. In his dissent in the infamous 1896 case, *Plessy v.*

Ferguson, Justice John Marshall Harlan writes that 'the real meaning' of segregated train carriages is that 'colored citizens are so inferior and degraded that they cannot be allowed to sit in public coaches occupied by white citizens' (*Plessy v. Ferguson* [1896], 560; cited in Eisgruber and Sager 2007, p. 128). Similarly, in his defence of *Brown v. Board of Education* [1954] and related cases, Charles Black writes of the 'plain fact' that in the United States 'the social meaning of segregation is the putting of the Negro in a position of walled-off inferiority' (Black 1960, p. 427). Jim Crow laws manifestly express racist attitudes, so a blanket scepticism about the possibility of objective social meaning is unwarranted. Some criterion of correct interpretation must be set out, but there is at least one case where facts about expressive meaning should not be doubted. Similarly, the unambiguous message of inferiority conveyed by Jim Crow legislation is a profound affront to the dignity and status of African-Americans. Anderson and Pildes (2000, pp. 1542–1543) argue that the stigmatic harm asserted in the Court's segregation and anti-miscegenation cases does not turn on evidence of feelings of inferiority or low self-esteem. Instead, the objection is that laws enforcing racial segregation directly injure African-Americans by immediately constituting them as second-class citizens, independently of their pernicious psychological, sociological, and economic consequences. This objection would have the same force in circumstances where these consequences were happily averted (Koppelman 2001). The democratic conception supposes that the scope of the right to rule is set by the demands of citizens' equal status, and these demands need not correspond to the severity of the material burdens imposed by a public policy. A government is not morally entitled to 'heap indignities on people' (Anderson and Pildes 2000, p. 1543) just because it can have the right to rule in a manner that may disadvantage them in more tangible ways.

The endorsement test

The First Amendment to the United States Constitution states that 'Congress shall make no law respecting an establishment of religion'. The Fourteenth Amendment makes this prohibition applicable within each state (*Everson v. Board of Education* [1947], 8), and hence prohibits establishment at all levels of government. The main statement of post-war Establishment Clause doctrine is the three-prong test set out in *Lemon v. Kurtzman* [1971]: government actions must have a secular purpose, their primary effect may not be to advance or inhibit religion, and they must not involve the excessive entanglement of government with religious institutions. In her concurring opinion in *Lynch v. Donnelly* [1984], a case concerning the constitutionality of a Christmas crèche displayed by the city of Pawtucket, Justice Sandra Day O'Connor proposed a more specific formulation of the first two elements:

> The purpose prong of the *Lemon* test asks whether government's actual purpose is to endorse or disapprove of religion. The effect prong asks whether, irrespective of government's actual purpose, the practice under review in fact conveys a message of endorsement or disapproval. An affirmative answer to either question should render the challenged practice invalid. (690)

In the case in question, O'Connor argued that Pawtucket's intention was merely to celebrate Christmas as a public holiday (691), and that the display did not in effect convey any message of endorsement of Christianity to citizens (692–693). In *Allegheny County v. Greater Pittsburgh ACLU* [1989], however, the Court used O'Connor's endorsement test to rule against the prominent display of Christian symbols on the grand staircase of the county courthouse.

It is clearly contrary to the First Amendment for the state to compel religious belief and performance, but it is not obvious why the merely symbolic affirmation of religion should also be rejected as unconstitutional.[5] Two arguments premise the endorsement test on the value of equality. The first argument states that official religious endorsements violate equality by disparaging adherents of minority religions. This is the primary argument advanced by Eisgruber and Sager. They claim that state endorsement of a religious belief or tradition violates the principle that citizens may not be 'disvalued on account of the spiritual foundations of their important commitments and projects' (Eisgruber and Sager 2007, p. 4). Not all controversial government endorsements could plausibly denigrate dissenting citizens. If Fineville were to declare itself a nuclear-free community, Eisgruber and Sager imagine, this would merely reflect the political attitude of the majority and would not deprecate inhabitants who favour nuclear energy (p. 124). In contrast, 'public endorsements of religion carry a special charge or valence' (p. 126). If Fineville were to declare itself a Christian community, the insulting message sent to its non-Christian inhabitants would be clear (p. 124). The difference between the two public declarations lies, they believe, in religion's distinctive sociology. Membership in a religion is constituted by assent to a comprehensive system of beliefs and by participation in various associated practices (p. 125). Religious affiliation is typically a matter of fundamental importance to a person. It determines her civic identity – who she is to herself and to others – in a way that political and other beliefs do not (p. 126). In affirming a religious claim, Eisgruber and Sager argue, the state implicitly denigrates the beliefs of other religious traditions. In denigrating these beliefs, government implicitly disparages those citizens who affirm them (p. 62). Official endorsements of other kinds of controversial beliefs do not have this implication insofar as these beliefs are not typically constitutive of a person's civic identity.[6]

The argument from disparagement is best understood as an expressivist argument. Eisgruber and Sager claim that the unconstitutional nature of official religious endorsements is contingent on sociological facts about religion, but not on the subjective attitudes that citizens have about such actions. Public officials may inadvertently demean adherents of minority religions (Eisgruber and Sager 2007, p. 127), and overly sensitive citizens may take offence at entirely constitutional government action (pp. 126, 135). Eisgruber and Sager claim that whether or not government action violates the Establishment Clause is determined by its objective social meaning (pp. 19, 124–128, 130–131). 'The social meaning of an event or a public expression is the meaning that a competent participant in the society in question would see in that event or expression' (p. 127). A public display of religious imagery expresses an endorsement of religion if the properly informed and competent members of the community would regard it as such. In the context of a society in which religious affiliation is constitutive of civic identity, the social meaning of such endorsements includes an attitude of disparagement (p. 131). Nonconformist minorities are stigmatised by the state's communication of its official disfavour and thereby constituted as kind of a pariah class. The imposition of this status is in itself a cognisable harm (p. 163), quite apart from whatever other infringements of constitutional rights it may bring out.

The second argument states that religious endorsements violate equality by excluding adherents of minority religions from genuine membership in the polity. This is the primary argument advanced by Nussbaum. She believes that the proclamation of an official creed would create a two-tier system of citizenship with members of religious minorities ranked below the majority (Nussbaum 2008, pp. 2, 74, 226–227). Religious orthodoxy is essentially hierarchical because it constitutes nonconformist minorities as outsiders rather than as full members of the community. In associating the state with a particular doctrine, establishment dissociates those who reject that doctrine from the polity. However integrated they may be in the daily life of the society, dissenting minorities will be defined by the fact of an official creed as deviant or marginal members of the public and hence as second-class citizens. Justice O'Connor writes that an official endorsement of religion 'sends a message to nonadherents that they are outsiders, not full members of the political community, and an accompanying message to adherents that they are insiders, favored members of the political community' (*Lynch v. Donnelly* [1984], 688). This message violates the basic First Amendment principle that government may not make 'adherence to a religion relevant in any way to a person's standing in the political community' (687).[7]

The argument from exclusion is also best understood as an expressivist argument. Anderson and Pildes (2000, p. 1550) claim that religious endorsements express an exclusive conception of membership in the polity. 'Citizens acting together through the State are already regarding nonadherents as outsiders when they endorse religion', quite apart from the cultural impact this may have (p. 1548). Nussbaum claims that an exclusionary hierarchy is 'a meaning expressed in the very fact of [religious] establishment' and not simply an effect it may often bring about (Nussbaum 2008, p. 85). The communication of this attitude through the creation of a religious orthodoxy 'is a statement that creates an in-group and an out-group' (p. 2) and 'immediately makes outsiders unequal' (p. 11). Even purely symbolic government endorsements of religion can marginalise (p. 81) and subordinate (p. 22): 'a failure of respect in the symbolic domain is like an insult, a slap in the face [of the sort] that a noble gives a vassal, one that both expresses and constitutes a hierarchy of ranks' (p. 226).

If either of the two arguments is successful, then the constitutional establishment of an official religion violates both principles of the democratic conception of legitimacy. The principle of equal respect requires that the state not express disparaging or exclusionary attitudes towards religious minorities, and the principle of equal standing requires that they not be subordinated in the public realm by an official stigmatisation or marginalisation. Consequently, although the two arguments are raised within the context of the American constitutional tradition, they are relevant to the political status of religion in any diverse society. Eisgruber and Sager limit the scope of their discussion to the United States, but the sociological features of religion they identity are by no means uniquely American. Since they claim that religious endorsements have a disparaging social meaning in virtue of these sociological features, their argument has much broader potential implications than their discussion suggests. Nussbaum, in contrast, explicitly argues that the American tradition of religious equality should guide other liberal democracies (Nussbaum 2008, pp. 13–14, 18). She claims that the separation of church and state is an essential element of equality precisely because religion is of fundamental importance to people. 'If religion were trivial, it would not be so vitally important to forestall hierarchies of status and freedom in religious matters' (p. 12). Thus, religious establishment could only be legitimate in unusual societies 'where people do not care very much about religion' (p. 13).[8]

The expressive meaning of religious endorsements

My contention is that the two arguments fail to show that the constitutional establishment of a majority religion is inevitably illegitimate in normal liberal societies. Whether a state's endorsement of an official religious doctrine expresses an attitude of disparagement or exclusion cannot be determined without examining a number of contextual factors, including the actual attitudes and commitments of the religion's adherents. This means that the expressive meaning of an official endorsement of a religion turns, inter alia, on the characteristics of the *specific* creed in question, as it is lived and practised in that context, and not on the *general* sociological features of religious identity common to all normal liberal societies. As a consequence, no sweeping generalisation about the illegitimate expressive meaning of religious establishment can be sustained. Indeed, there are sometimes reasons to be more sceptical of the legitimacy of symbolic endorsements of religion in unusual societies where people are largely indifferent to religious values.

If the two arguments are to succeed, the state's explicit attitude about a particular *creed* must imply an implicit attitude about the *adherents* of other faiths. Without this implication, the claim that the establishment of the majority religion disrespects or subordinates religious minorities is unsubstantiated. The two arguments therefore require a proper response to the indeterminacy challenge. Without a clear criterion for the correct interpretation of a law's objective social meaning, no implicit attitude about people can be inferred from an explicit attitude about a doctrine. Eisgruber and Sager's (2007, p. 127) 'competent participant' proposal cannot provide an adequate criterion for two reasons. First, the competent members of a community will clearly disagree about whether an attitude of disparagement or exclusion is part of the social meaning of a government action. Thus, expressive meaning cannot be 'like linguistic meaning' (p. 127).[9] Second, the proposal does not offer the members of the community any normative guidance in their interpretation of government action, since it just says that the social meaning of an action is what they think it is. Deborah Hellman's suggestion that the 'expressive dimension of a law or policy is best understood as the meaning that we would arrive at if we were to discuss the interpretive question together under fair conditions' (Hellman 2000, p. 23) is unsatisfactory for the same reason. No subjunctive claim about how certain deliberators would interpret a policy can constitute an adequate criterion of correct interpretation since such a claim says nothing about the features of the policy in virtue of which it has a particular expressive meaning.

At least two elements should figure in any criterion of expressive meaning. First, for an action to express an attitude, there must be some connection between the attitude and the best explanation of the action's actual performance. Anderson and Pildes (2000, p. 1510) claim that an action expresses an attitude if the agent acts on the reasons that the attitude provides. The determination of expressive meaning thus depends on a judgment about which purposes best explain the action. These need not be conscious purposes (p. 1513). For instance, Alice may express a desire to exclude Boris from a conversation by talking loudly over him, without being consciously aware of that desire. Second, an action may express an attitude if that attitude makes rational sense of the agent acting as she does for the reasons she does in the context she inhabits. Alice's exclusion of Boris expresses inconsiderateness towards her other interlocutors, even though this is not her purpose, if her action is rationally coherent only insofar as she is indifferent to or oblivious of their desire to keep him in the conversation (pp. 1512–1513).

Government action is more complex than individual action since the proponents of a policy do not usually support it for the same set of reasons. However, not every set of reasons determines a policy's expressive meaning. If the idiosyncratic rationales of isolated legislators do not actually explain why a law was enacted, then they need not figure as attitudes expressed by the law. Despite the greater complexity of collective decision making, it is often possible to identify certain predominant purposes that explain why the policy was adopted. To fix ideas, consider Jim Crow restrictions on the use of public facilities. To be unable to sit on a park bench or drink from a water foundation is, in itself, a very minor inconvenience, but to be barred on grounds of race is to be treated with contempt as an inferior. On the face of it, this is a quite dramatic inference, one that may be unsupported by any explicit assertion of racial inferiority in public signs or the legislative record. But even in the unlikely event that the legislators were not themselves consciously motivated by racism, any explanation of the restrictions' existence in that historical context must invoke their function in a broader social system of racial domination (Black 1960, pp. 424–427). This function is therefore one of the predominant purposes of the laws. Since acting for the purpose of maintaining racial domination makes rational sense only insofar as one endorses white supremacist convictions, Jim Crow legislation expresses profoundly illegitimate racist attitudes.

The ascription of expressive meaning to government action thus turns on two theses: a claim about the predominant purposes that best explain the performance of the government action, and a claim about the best rational reconstruction of the government's acting as it does, for those purposes, in a particular political context. Insofar as these theses can be objectively supported, the claim that a government action can have an objective social meaning is warranted.[10] Perhaps some government actions have no determinate expressive meaning because one or other of the two theses cannot be made out. This possibility is quite compatible with the expressivist analysis of democratic legitimacy, as far as it goes, since it only implies that it is sometimes indeterminate whether a government action expresses illegitimate attitudes.

My account of the expressive meaning of government action demonstrates why some symbolic endorsements of religion can violate the democratic conception, even in unusual societies where few people are religious. Consider a variant of Eisgruber and Sager's Fineville example. Suppose that the city council of Eliteville decides to erect a very expensive statue of the founding figure of the majority's religion, with the creed's commandments carved into the plinth. However, almost all people in Eliteville, including the members of the city council, are indifferent to religious doctrine and make no effort to live in accordance with the dictates of their nominal faiths. Religious services are poorly attended and the few professional clerics resident in the town are well-known for their agnostic inclinations and secular sensibilities. The purpose of the statue would then be quite puzzling: why should the majority of the townspeople support, at great cost, the symbolic affirmation of a religion that they disregard in their daily lives? One solution to this puzzle would be available if religious affiliation generally tracked a quite different social division. In this case, religious affiliation need not itself be an important constituent of civic identity, but it may by accident of history be a good indicator of the social categories that are. For instance, suppose that the members of the majority denomination in the town are overwhelmingly part of an ethnic elite, one that has historically used force to maintain its dominant position in the society. The erection of the statue might then be best explained as a signal to members of other ethnic groups to keep to their subservient place. In this context, the city council's symbolic affirmation of the majority's traditional creed makes most rational sense as a thin façade for an attitude of ethnic chauvinism at odds with equal respect. Since no government entity can have the moral right to express this hostile attitude towards citizens, the statue's expressive meaning violates the democratic conception. Should the statue be dismantled by the national government, or even destroyed in a dramatic act of civil disobedience, the moral right of the townspeople to decide how best to use public funds would not be infringed. To the extent that the city council has exceeded its legitimate authority, it is not morally entitled to any deference.

Establishment without inequality

The constitutional establishment of a religious doctrine can have a much greater effect on a society's institutions and its citizens' rights than any symbolic display. It does not follow, however, that the case against religious constitutional establishment is easier to make than the case against Eliteville's statue. Consider a society in which the constitution explicitly confers an official status on the majority religion and makes some of its tenets legally binding.[11] Suppose that the public consumption of alcohol is restricted because the religion defines inebriation as an affront to the dignity of the human soul; elective abortion and assisted suicide are prohibited as contrary to the divine sanctity of life; and no person may deliberately harm the religion's sacred animal. The official status of the religion allows public schools to teach its account of the creation of the universe and the origin of human life alongside competing scientific accounts. These provisions are presumably at odds with the best liberal theory of justice and education. Since the right to rule allows some range of unjust and unwise public policies, however, it does not follow that they are illegitimate. The basic civil and political rights of religious minorities are otherwise guaranteed, and anti-discrimination laws are stringently enforced.

Suppose that the majority of citizens in the religious republic, unlike those in Eliteville, are sincere in their commitment to their faith. The purpose of the establishment would then not be especially puzzling. It is unsurprising that people would support state affirmation of principles and doctrines they believe to be of great significance. There is no need here to invoke any incidental social antagonism to explain the constitution's religious content. The predominant purpose of the establishment is not to shore up a system of ethnic domination or class privilege, but rather to give effect to some of the religion's tenets in the public domain. The constitutional enforcement of these requirements is necessary, the majority believe, because majoritarian legislation with the same purpose would be struck down by the judiciary as a violation of individual rights to self-determination. Without some clear constitutional provisions, the majority would be powerless to prevent acts their religion defines as morally abhorrent or to allow the teaching of claims they believe to be true. Their motivation is analogous to that of citizens who seek to enact constitutional amendments prohibiting flag-burning or racist hate speech, with the exception that the content of the relevant norms is explicitly religious.

Members of religious minorities and secular liberals may find the provisions offensive and insulting. Nevertheless, the expressive meaning of a law is not determined by the subjective attitudes that citizens have towards it (Anderson and Pildes 2000, p. 1524). If the provisions are illegitimate on expressivist grounds, this must be because their objective social meaning is inconsistent with equal status. The religious purpose of the establishment must rationally imply an attitude of disparagement or exclusion towards religious minorities. But whether this is the case turns on quite specific contextual features, ones that are not generally present in normal societies where religious affiliation is constitutive of civic identity.

Consider each argument in turn. Eisgruber and Sager (2007, pp. 62, 131) claim that in endorsing a religion, the state disparages adherents of other creeds. But a *state's* affirmation of a doctrine must then be quite unlike an *individual's* affirmation of that doctrine. It is clearly possible for individuals to subscribe to a religious doctrine in a manner that expresses contempt for followers of other faiths. History is replete with pious bigots who have held themselves superior to the unrighteous heretics in their midst. Religious establishments that are best explained by appeal to the sincere bigotry of the majority are illegitimate. But if all instances of religious affirmation were like this, then mutual denigration would be an ineliminable feature of any diverse liberal society. Instead, it is commonplace for individuals to subscribe to a set of religious convictions without denigrating or disvaluing the identities of people who reject those convictions. Liberal religious adherents can even celebrate the diversity of religious traditions without any particular desire that others convert to the true faith. Nor does partiality to one's own creed imply an improper partiality towards its adherents. Thus, neutrality in religious matters is not required for individuals to demonstrate an equitable respect for their fellow citizens, even given the close sociological connection between religious conviction and civic identity.

Assume, then, that the majority espouse their theology in a relatively liberal manner. Bigotry has no place in the moral content of the established religion or in the attitudes of its adherents. They do not hold themselves generally superior to adherents of other religions and do not regard them as benighted fools who stubbornly resist seeing the light. Members of the majority do not shun social contact with nonconformist citizens, nor do they prefer to live in segregated neighborhoods or send their children to segregated schools. In this context, an individual's affirmation of the majority religion does not express any objectionable attitude of disparagement or denigration towards those with quite different beliefs. The culture of the society does not itself attach any stigma to religious difference. Some members of religious minorities might want to engage in activities the majority regard as abhorrent – the consumption of alcohol and the flesh of the sacred animal, for instance. Although the minority do not share the religious belief that these practices are abhorrent, the majority religion need not include any moral injunction against erroneous convictions: it is profoundly wrong to assist in suicide, but it is not at all wrong to believe that suicide is morally acceptable or to wish to help end a loved one's suffering. Again, some such distinction between the ethics of acts and the ethics of moral attitudes is commonplace.

What is needed for the argument from disparagement to succeed is some explanation for why the different nature of the agent affirming the doctrine – the state rather than private individuals and associations – should introduce an entirely *new attitude* into the meaning of the affirmation. This is not to ask why it can make a moral difference for different kinds of agent to express the *same attitude*. Individuals have the moral right to express contempt for each other in a way that a government does not since a government can subordinate citizens in the public realm in a way that individuals cannot. Instead, the problem is to explain why an attitude of disparagement is expressed in the state's espousal of a doctrine if that attitude is not already expressed in the majority's espousal of the same doctrine in the same social context. Nothing precludes this possibility, but arguments that merely identify the distinctive sociological and cultural features of religious affiliation and the great importance that religious convictions typically have for individuals cannot provide a sufficient explanation. These arguments may demonstrate some difference between a government's endorsement of a religious doctrine and its endorsement of a controversial policy about nuclear power. But they cannot by themselves demonstrate any difference between individual and state espousal of a controversial religious doctrine, since the *same* sociological features cut across both these cases. There is therefore a lacuna in the argument from disparagement that some further consideration must bridge.

The argument from exclusion presents a somewhat sharper challenge to the democratic legitimacy of religious establishment since it is compatible with the assumption that the majority do not denigrate the identities of religious minorities. The argument does not suppose that the state subordinates religious minorities by placing its imprimatur on any existing cultural stigma. Instead, it supposes only that in establishing an official religion, the constitution defines the polity as a community united by a common faith. This definition implies that those who reject that faith are not genuine members of the polity, no matter how well-regarded they may otherwise be. Since they are constituted as outsiders, they do not enjoy an equal status with the majority. Religious establishment therefore subordinates through marginalisation, the argument concludes, quite apart from any morally objectionable attitudes towards the minority that adherents of the official religion may already have.

The key premise in the argument from exclusion is that the objective social meaning of religious establishment includes a definition of the polity as a community of the faithful. But this meaning cannot be inferred from the official status of the religion by itself. The state must officially endorse a great many controversial views, but does not ipso facto define the polity as a community united in consensus on those views. When a democratic government endorses a belief about the threat of global warming, for instance, it treats climate change sceptics not as outsiders but simply as a mistaken minority. Whether the constitutional establishment of a religious doctrine has an exclusionary expressive meaning depends on the precise nature of its purpose. This requires an examination, not only of the moral attitudes of the majority, but also of which aspects of the philosophical content of the religion find expression through its official status.

Suppose that the theological doctrine of the majority religion distinguishes between two kinds of moral norm: *identity-neutral* norms apply to all persons whereas *identity-specific* norms apply only to adherents of the religion itself. For instance, if the religion teaches that any person who lies or cheats has acted immorally, it regards honesty and fairness as identity-neutral norms. In contrast, a duty to fast or to dress in a certain manner may be identity-specific norms. Adherents of other faiths do not act immorally if they do not fast or if they dress in a different fashion, since these duties arise only in virtue of a person's commitment to the religion.[12] The distinction between the two kinds of norm concerns which agents are bound by the relevant requirements and not the moral epistemology of the norms. Identity-neutral norms are not universal in scope because they can be independently derived within all reasonable moral traditions. Some may be justifiable in this manner, but other identity-neutral norms will presuppose key elements of the religious doctrine. In such cases, there is something wrong in anyone acting contrary to the norm even if not all reasonable people can be expected to accept this. The norm may simply be revealed in scripture as God's will for all human beings, and therefore depend for its cogency on the truth of the religion's core premises. Thus, identity-neutral norms need not be freestanding in Rawls's (2005, p. 12) sense of the term.

Whether the fact of an established religion defines the polity as a community of the faithful depends on how the two kinds of moral norm feature in its political life. Suppose that the religion's prohibition of alcohol, abortion, and suicide are identity-specific moral norms. In this case, the government presupposes the established religion, not only in the moral justification of its policies, but also as part of the identity of citizens. If the purpose of the restrictions is to ensure that citizens as such respect moral duties that they could only have as adherents of the official religion, then the state expresses the attitude that citizens as such are supposed to be members of the faith. Moreover, even if the state were to exempt religious minorities from all identity-specific prohibitions, the very fact of these prohibitions would likely indicate an especial concern for the ethical lives of the majority. Since this concern could only be justified by a further identity-specific norm – such as the responsibility of a congregation to care for the moral standing of its members – the state would act on the basis of a conception of the polity as a community of the faithful. Similar instances of government actions that are best rationalised by identity-specific norms would support the argument from exclusion's interpretation of the society's religious establishment.

A quite contrary interpretation would be supported, however, if the state were scrupulous in observing the distinction between the two kinds of norm. Assume that each constitutional and legal provision justified by the established doctrine is grounded in some or other identity-neutral norm. Thus, the religion teaches that all persons are morally bound to respect the dignity of their souls and the sanctity of life, and that its account of creation is an objective truth about the universe. The corresponding provisions do not, therefore, express any implicit assumption about the religious identity of genuine citizens. Moreover, no laws aim at ensuring that members of the majority live in accordance with their identity-specific religious obligations. In this case, the government regards certain religious principles as binding in politics, but not in virtue of any definition of the polity as a community united in commitment to those principles. The purpose of the establishment is simply to ensure the political protection of certain values and truths that the majority take to be compelling. Even if the majority believe this because of their commitment to a doctrine that is constitutive of their identities, it does not follow that the state's endorsement of the same doctrine is similarly constitutive of the identity of the polity. The religious basis for their political views implies only that, as a democratic majority, they are in a condition of intractable disagreement with a political minority, and not that they are marginalising them as outsiders. Such an interpretation of the establishment's expressive meaning would exceed what can be objectively supported by the best explanation of its underlying purpose and the attitudes that are required to make rational sense of the state acting on this purpose. Objectivity cuts both ways. There is no reason to presume that an expressivist analysis is more likely to indict than it is to vindicate the legitimacy of contested government practices.

Conclusion

In this paper, I have argued that the expressive meaning of some official endorsements of religion is compatible with the democratic conception of legitimacy. It does not follow that O'Connor's endorsement test should be restricted to those instances where government action does in fact convey a message of disparagement or exclusion. The endorsement test is a criterion of constitutionality in the United States and not a criterion of political legitimacy. Although these two kinds of norms are closely connected, they must be kept distinct; the one does not always imply the other.

First, not every requirement of political legitimacy is properly enforced by the judiciary. I have claimed that legislators have no moral right to enact a law just so that their personal property increases in value. To do so would violate the principle of equal respect, since the legislators would privilege their own interests above those of other citizens. This moral restriction on legislative discretion should guide legislators in their deliberations and should inform the reactive attitudes of citizens as they decide how to vote. But it does not follow that the judiciary should strike down the law, even if the constitution grants them the power to enforce its provisions against the will of the majority. Considered in itself – apart from the motivation of the legislators – the law may lie within the bounds of permissible state action. Moreover, the expressive meaning of a public policy can turn on information that judges are not well placed to discover in any timely fashion. Their decisions are often better guided by standards that only imperfectly satisfy the demands of equal status, especially if a more ambitious approach would likely foster excessive judicial intrusion in the democratic process. Constitutional norms are subject to the practical limitations of complex institutional arrangements to a degree that moral truths about political legitimacy are not.

Second, legitimate constitutional provisions can be much more demanding than the principles of democratic legitimacy. The Second Amendment to the United States Constitution guarantees the right to bear arms and the Twenty-Second Amendment prohibits anyone being elected president more than twice. Neither of these provisions is itself a requirement of political legitimacy; a society with no guns and no terms limits can satisfy the democratic conception with no difficulty. Similarly, the Establishment Clause of the First Amendment can have pluralistic foundations (Shiffrin 2004) in that its proper interpretation may turn on values and considerations in addition to the equal status of citizens. Moreover, although it is quite unlikely that official affirmations of religion in the specific social and cultural context of the United States would invariably express illegitimate attitudes, a prohibition of all such endorsements may be the best way to rule out the many that would. I am sympathetic to the claim that these considerations support the use of the endorsement test as a constitutional norm within the United States. But proponents of the test must not overstate the case for it. The quixotic search for illegitimate attitudes where none need exist simply discredits the entire expressivist approach to democratic legitimacy and constitutional interpretation.

Acknowledgements

An earlier version of this paper was presented at Tulane University during my tenure as a fellow at the Center for Ethics and Public Affairs in 2010–2011. I am grateful to the audience members on that occasion for their remarks and to the Center itself for providing a wonderful research environment. I am also grateful to Shaun Bockert, Emanuela Ceva, Andrew Garland and Enzo Rossi for their written comments on an earlier draft.

Notes

1. I take up the formulation and defence of a principle of secular public justification in a separate project. A third question, in addition to the problems of political legitimacy and public justification, concerns whether the ethics of democratic citizenship precludes essentially religious argumentation in public deliberation.
2. It follows that the right to rule is a complex instance of the right to do wrong (Waldron 1981). I defend this claim in a separate project, and simply acknowledge here that it is not uncontroversial.
3. Although it is implausible that citizens have a very strong duty to obey every legitimate law, there are clearly some strong moral duties correlative to the right to rule. If the general staff of the military forces refused to allow a democratically elected politician to be inaugurated as president, they would violate a moral duty they owe to both her and to the electorate. The president-elect has acquired a right to take office, and this right includes a strong moral claim against others that they not prevent her from doing so.
4. I have criticised Rawls's liberal principle in May (2009). For another substantive theory of legitimacy that includes reciprocity as a core democratic value, in addition to equality and political autonomy, see Brettschneider (2007).
5. A more permissive Establishment Clause test finds expression in *Lee v. Weisman*, a 1992 case concerning the constitutionality of a religious invocation and benediction at a public high school graduation ceremony. Writing for the majority, Justice Anthony Kennedy found that the school in effect compelled participation in a religious exercise (*Lee v. Weisman* [1992], 594–596, 598). What matters for Kennedy's coercion test is not whether the state places its

imprimatur on religion, but whether public officials exploit the intimidating power of the state to proselytise.

6. Nussbaum (2008) also accepts the argument from disparagement. She claims that Christian establishment would degrade non-Christians (p. 92) and that the public display of the Ten Commandments denigrates Hindus, Buddhists, and other non-monotheists (p. 269).
7. Eisgruber and Sager (2007) also accept the argument from exclusion (pp. 122–123). They write that public endorsements of religion contain a 'message of exclusion' (p. 156) and define minorities as outsiders (pp. 126, 130, 163).
8. In a separate work, Nussbaum (2000, pp. 210–211) claims that it is a 'contingent contextual question' whether the various important capabilities of citizens are best protected through a secular state or 'a regime of limited establishment with sufficient safeguards for citizen equality and free exercise.' I endorse a similar contextual approach to the evaluation of the legitimacy of religious establishment, so it may seem as if I am arguing against the wrong target. Such an objection would be misplaced, however. First, my concern in this paper is simply with the implications of the arguments from disparagement and exclusion, and not with the overall views of any particular theorist as such. Second, Nussbaum's claim is that religious establishment may be better than the only available secular alternatives, if these would violate the equality of religious minorities in more egregious ways. For instance, she claims that India's 'limited plural establishment' forestalls a threat to the religious liberty and equality of Muslim citizens, and that 'total nonestablishment would be de facto a type of Hindu establishment' (pp. 211, also pp. 214–230). There is no claim here that the constitutional establishment of a majority religion could be just as legitimate as an entirely innocuous secular regime.
9. Anderson and Pildes (2000, pp. 1565–1570) reject the conflation of expressive meaning with linguistic meaning present in Matthew Adler's critique of expressivism (Adler 2000). Actions can clearly express attitudes without the agent having any intention to communicate these attitudes.
10. My account here departs somewhat from the account of collective attitudes presented by Anderson and Pildes. They claim that a group has a mental state if and only if its members are jointly committed to expressing that mental state as a body (Anderson and Pildes 2000, p. 1517). As Simon Blackburn observes, however, this stipulation is in tension with the claim that agents need not be consciously aware of the attitudes they express (Blackburn 2001, pp. 474–476).
11. This example draws on one I have advanced in May (2009).
12. In some cases, a moral norm may even be mixed. The religion might assert that all people should help the poor, but that this is especially incumbent upon followers of the true faith.

References

Adler, M. D., 2000. Expressive theories of law: a skeptical overview. *University of Pennsylvania Law Review*, 148 (5), 1363–1501.

Allegheny County v. Greater Pittsburgh ACLU [1989] 492 US 573.

Anderson, E. S. and Pildes, R. H., 2000. Expressive theories of law: a general restatement. *University of Pennsylvania Law Review*, 148 (5), 1503–1575.

Black, C. L., 1960. The lawfulness of the segregation decisions. *Yale Law Journal*, 69 (3), 421–430.

Blackburn, S., 2001. Group minds and expressive harm. *Maryland Law Review*, 60 (3), 467–491.

Brettschneider, C., 2007. *Democratic rights: the substance of self-government*. Princeton, NJ: Princeton University Press.

Brown v. Board of Education [1954] 347 US 483.

Buchanan, A., 2004. *Justice, legitimacy, and self-determination: moral foundations for international law*. Oxford: Oxford University Press.

Christiano, T., 2008. *The constitution of equality: democratic authority and its limits*. Oxford: Oxford University Press.

Copp, D., 1999. The idea of a legitimate state. *Philosophy and Public Affairs*, 28 (1), 3–45.

Eisgruber, C. and Sager, L., 2007. *Religious freedom and the constitution*. Cambridge, MA: Harvard University Press.

Everson v. Board of Education [1947] 330 US 1.

Hellman, D., 2000. The expressive dimension of equal protection. *Minnesota Law Review*, 80 (1), 1–69.

Koppelman, A., 2001. On the moral foundations of legal expressivism. *Maryland Law Review*, 60 (3), 777–784.

Lee v. Weisman [1992] 505 US 577.

Lemon v. Kurtzman [1971] 403 US 602.

Lynch v. Donnelly [1984] 465 US 668.

May, S. C., 2009. Religious democracy and the liberal principle of legitimacy. *Philosophy and Public Affairs*, 37 (2), 136–170.

Nussbaum, M., 2000. *Women and human development*. Cambridge: Cambridge University Press.

Nussbaum, M., 2008. *Liberty of conscience. in defense of America's tradition of religious equality*. New York, NY: Basic Books.

Plessy v. Ferguson [1896] 163 US 537.

Rawls, J., 2005. *Political liberalism*. New York, NY: Columbia University Press.

Shiffrin, S. H., 2004. The pluralistic foundations of the religion clauses. *Cornell Law Review*, 90 (1), 9–95.

Simmons, A. J., 1999. Justification and legitimacy. *Ethics*, 109 (4), 739–771.

Waldron, J., 1981. A right to do wrong. *Ethics*, 92 (1), 21–39.

Global justification and local legitimation

Sebastiano Maffettone

LUISS University, Rome, Italy

This paper distinguishes between the concepts of justification and legitimation with a view to offering a normative standard for global justice compatible with cultural pluralism. According to this distinction, justification is presented as an idealized, substantive and top-down enterprise rooted in the moral and metaphysical substrate of a specific culture. On the other hand, legitimation has a procedural and factual connotation and derives its strength from the success of some culturally independent but historically situated practice (bottom-up approach). Building on this distinction, I argue that justification and legitimation should be made complementary for the sake of cross-cultural dialogue.

Introduction

According to G. W. F. Hegel, the history of philosophy aims at the formulation of a dialectic through which the absoluteness of the spirit becomes embedded in all the cultures that have reflectively existed. This apparent pluralism of forms of life is however contradicted by Hegel's philosophy of history in which the world history is viewed as a normative progression of stages, developing from its Oriental beginning to its German–Christian fulfilment.[1] This tension between cultural historicity and pluralism on the one hand and a Western-centric philosophy of history on the other has been emphasized among others by many post-colonial critics of Hegel (Chakrabatry 2011). On this basis, post-colonial critics of Hegel often maintain that any reconciliation between reason and history must be considered both implausible and morally wrong because it is founded on the highly controversial and Western-centric Hegelian philosophy of history.

The nihilist approach implicit in post-colonial philosophies tends to block any reasonable attempt to reconcile cultural pluralism with the aspiration to have common global principles of justice (Maffettone 2011). For this reason, many scholars have rejected both Hegel's imperialistic approach to philosophy of history as well as the post-colonial relativistic reaction to it. Among these are certainly John Rawls (Rawls 1993) and Jürgen Habermas (Habermas 1992), on whose ideas, among others, I rely in this article. In fact, my own arguments can be included in the vast array of post-Hegelian attempts to reconcile pluralism and universalism with an eye to world history. More precisely, I present a theoretical model that seeks to make cultural pluralism compatible with global justice.

The mention of Hegel was meant to show that global justice and cultural pluralism are topics that can be discussed from a variety of perspectives. However, my specific take on global justice is distinctively liberal. This may be a source of puzzlement to some, given the Western origins of liberalism. However, I have decided to go this way in light of what I take to be the twofold nature of liberal political theory. On the one hand, liberalism may be conceived as a comprehensive doctrine and in this sense it is certainly incompatible with a cross-cultural, pluralistic perspective (call this liberalism1). On the other hand, liberalism may be viewed as a meta-theoretical device arguing for a political consensus compatible with a plurality of comprehensive doctrines (call this liberalism2). Therefore, from the perspective of liberalism2, cross-cultural dialogue is not only permitted but encouraged (as a consequence of pluralism; Rawls 1993).

A second specification regards the idea of human rights I employ: the fundamental human rights recognized in the *Universal Declaration of Human Rights* (1948) and related *Covenants* (1966 and the following) as a standard of an already existing, (partially) shared cross-cultural point of view at the global level. This is made possible by the theoretical distinction I make between justification and legitimation.

My main argument is that, by referring to fundamental human rights interpreted coherently with liberalism2, we can improve the standards of cross-cultural dialogue in the domain of global justice to make it more hospitable to cultural pluralism. I build on the idea that (philosophical) justifications are always connoted in cultural terms. Accordingly, given the fact of cultural pluralism, reasonable dissent on justifications and their standards is unavoidable. In other words, philosophical justification presupposes some shared cultural background, from which the reasons offered in support of a certain view are drawn. I draw this in part from Rawls (1971, 1993), according to whom justification – unlike demonstration – relies on shared premises. These premises are embedded in local cultures. So, for example, a Western liberal would find it difficult to convince through philosophical justification a committed Hindu that Western-like secularization is an intrinsic good, as they would lack a shared cultural background for appreciating each other's reasons. This is why we also need what I call legitimation: a recognized practice or a public experience of historical success on which there exists widespread agreement. Legitimation, so conceived, is institutional and the agreement it implies happens only within a limited range of institutional matters. The constitutional history of a liberal-democratic polity offers a standard example of how shared legitimation may be reached starting with different cultural justifications. So, for instance, the cultural background of a US citizen can be African-American, Latino or European, but s/he can nonetheless comply with and have trust for the US Constitution and the ensuing political form of life.

My hunch is that people around the world can experience a similar loyalty when they face cross-cultural problems of justice at the global level. I claim, however, that at the global level the standard of legitimation cannot be the same that is at work in a liberal democracy. It should rather consist in a reference to fundamental human rights. So I submit that people endorsing different standards of cultural justification compatible with what I have called liberalism2 – including, for example, a Rawlsian ideal of the liberal society or a post-Confucian ideal of harmonious society – can nevertheless converge on the same limited set of legally existing human rights even if they do so for different ethical and metaphysical reasons. The result I hope to obtain is admittedly modest: only if one believes in liberalism as pluralism (liberalism2) and is confident about the general acceptability of certain basic human rights, s/he will regard my claim as plausible.

My argument unfolds as follows. I start by clarifying my distinction between legitimation and justification. On this basis, I suggest an interpretation of human rights as a global practice compatible with the idea of legitimation. I then move onto presenting my proposal of what I call 'pluralist integration from below'. From this perspective, the reasons supporting the justification of fundamental human rights must be rooted in different cultural traditions. With this proposal on the table, I make use of the idea of a Rawls-inspired overlapping consensus between different cultural foundations of fundamental human rights. Reaching an overlapping consensus, however, presupposes a shared basic structure (Rawls 1993, lectures IV, VI). In this light I discuss the idea of the basic structure as the site of justice with an eye to the scope and the ground of justice.

With these conceptual clarifications in place, I turn to the main issue of the article: cultural pluralism and global justice. How can we export the Rawlsian model of an overlapping consensus beyond the nation-state? How can we make up for the absence of a global basic structure? In my view, generally accepted legal documents establishing universal human rights can play this function. The remainder of the paper is devoted to substantiating this claim by building on the complementary nature of justification and legitimation. I distinguish between two different kinds of justification, labelled respectively 'universal' and 'special'. And, in order not to disappoint fans of symmetry, I distinguish also between two kinds of legitimation, labelled respectively 'general' and 'local'. My conclusion tries to make sense of this abstract machinery and to argue that it represents a good premise and a reasonable promise for historical cross-cultural dialogue.

Justification and legitimation

Justification and legitimation usually overlap in the writings of political theorists, but I think it important to distinguish between them.[2] For me, in brief, justification consists in the search for the best theoretical argument in support to some view, is intrinsically substantive, goes top-down, and is rooted in the moral and metaphysical bases of a specific culture. Legitimation, on the other hand, is normally based on an institutional practice, concerns mainly the inputs of a political process, goes bottom up, and does not directly appeal to the moral and metaphysical roots of a culture. Thus characterized, justification and legitimation are complementary: given the fact of cultural pluralism, different plausible justifications may conflict with each other, but we can nonetheless rely on the same institutional practices of legitimation.

The idea of justification I presented may be regarded as rather standard, as it may be translated into the idea that a view should win only when it is supported by the force of the best normative argument. This view of justification must be conceived of in terms of cultural pluralism. My idea of legitimation is admittedly more unusual. By legitimation I mean a specific, widely recognized practice through which institutional legitimacy is conferred. Legitimation-conferring practices may operate at two separate levels: locally (their object would be the society's main institutions) or globally (their object would be, for example, some international treaty). In either case practices of legitimation are open to contextual variations, but while at the local level it may well be possible that the standard legitimation practice, in say, Sudan, is different from that in the United States (due to cultural components of the different relevant contexts), the legitimation of an existing global practice such as human rights is connoted in intercultural terms. Divorce between justification and legitimation cannot be durable. On the one hand, a country may legitimate a dictator through consent – like, for example, Italy during Fascism – but after a while this unjustified legitimation fails to be acceptable. On the other hand, an intellectual or religious group can justify a norm different from an established legitimated practice but has no right (failing legitimation) to use public institutions against the general will.

Habermas made an implicit use of this distinction when he urged for a structural compromise between 'practical reason' and 'social praxis' (Habermas 1996). He assumes that validity claims of practical reason disconnected from factual reality. To avoid this form of abstraction, Habermas's critical theory enters the domain of positive law. In such a way, normativity tries to objectivate itself. The outcome should be the re-conjunction of the ideal validity of practical reason, which is normative and decontextualized, and social validity, which is on the contrary connected to the factual criteria of praxis. This re-conjunction requires the public recognition of the legal validity of democratic law, guaranteed by the equilibrium between the evidence of general legal compliance and the possibility to justify this compliance in reference to the dialogical nature of liberal-democracy. No complex contemporary society may be held together by the appeal to abstract normative values alone (practical reason), but it rather requires the complement of factually operating institutions like the market, democracy and the judicial power (praxis). In my view, this strategy is better explained through the cooperative force of justification and legitimation, as previously defined. Justification would provide the ethical content, while legitimation will be at the basis of the actual performance of a working system of rules.

Albeit with greater philosophical prudence, a similar move is shared by Rawls (1993). Rawls actually does not think in terms of a coherent integration between a normative–philosophical justification and a factual legitimation. Rather he works within the domain of a philosophical theory of justice. Nevertheless, he must concede that a pure philosophical justification of a liberal democracy is insufficient to guarantee the equilibrium between respect for pluralism and concern for stability. This is where the social device of an overlapping consensus between different comprehensive doctrines enters the scene. Within a well-ordered society, citizens with different comprehensive but reasonable views of the world can peacefully coexist with each other if they operate within the same shared political background (I shall revisit in greater detail Rawls's idea of an overlapping consensus below). This fortunate equilibrium is permitted by a successful constitutional history. The history of an empirical success, like that of the American constitution across time, becomes in such a way coherent with the ethical–political normative premises of the Rawlsian discourse. To translate this into my terminology, the philosophical justification offered by the principles of justice meets here the factual legitimation given by American public legal history.[3]

In the light of my proposed account, I submit that the existence of a just basic structure cannot depend exclusively on a theoretical justification. It must depend also on a successful model of institutional interaction. In brief, only a quasi-empirical notion of legitimation potentially unifies the structural pluralism of justifications under a coherent vision of justice. In sum, I submit that the conjunction of legitimation and justification constitutes the unification of a legal practice and an ethical project from the point of view of what I have elsewhere called normative institutionalism (Maffettone 2010, ch. 1). Justification is normative and comes from the ethical argument according to which we should find fair terms of cooperation among ourselves as citizens of a liberal democratic state. Legitimation is institutional and comes from the fact that liberal democracy is, in our age, a (relatively) successful practice. From the point of view of Rawls's normative institutionalism, liberal democracy is the only political regime capable of uniting justification and legitimation. And it is from this normative perspective which we are told what limits on pluralism are allowed: constitutional essentials and basic matters of justice constrain the possibilities of dissent because they are the foundations upon which the building of a liberal democracy is grounded. In this article, I am committed to using a similar argument but with a broader scope. In particular, I want to show how we can take human rights as source of legitimation when discussing global justice from a cultural pluralist point of view.

Human rights as a source of global legitimation

With the benefit of hindsight, the history of human rights is a success story (among others, see Glendon 2001). However, this has not always been the case. Quite the opposite: the affirmation of human rights has been a troubled process and only particular historical conditions allowed them to gain a relative legal and political effectiveness. It is historically unquestionable that it was the advent of Nazism and its military and ideological defeat which fostered the faith in human rights in the West. As matter of fact, in the West, before the Second World War, human rights were rather unpopular and Eastern countries were more ready to present them as an item in the global agenda.

It is complex to say in what sense – moral, rhetorical, legal – human rights can be altogether taken as a success story, as I said above. We can suggest that their success depends on the fact that 'the global human rights enterprise' (Beitz 2009, ch. 2) constitutes a widely accepted, even if not yet a 'mature' practice.[4] This practice offers a set of public rules for the behaviour of a class of significant global agents, beginning with nation-states. Moreover, it is normally thought – at least among the members of international organizations – that the rules provided by human rights should be complied with, and there are institutions and informal procedures for their implementation.

Throughout the years, the greatest theoretical resistance among theorists of international relations to the dominant paradigm based on human rights came from political realists, initially and cultural differentialists, at a later stage. In my view, notwithstanding the differences between realism (Cranston 1973) and differentialism (for which see in part Derrida in Cornell et al. 1992), both their criticisms of human rights focus on the idea that human rights impose a universalistic view incompatible with specific and localized needs and concerns. However, this shared objection is interpreted in extremely different ways: realists see such a universalism as an improper abstraction with respect to the actual mechanisms of the state that determine its political will and are connected to sovereignty. Differentialists, on the other hand, emphasize the inadequacy of a culture of human rights with respect to cultural diversity. There is much to be learned from criticisms of a dominant paradigm, and the subject of human rights is no exception to this general rule. The way out of the problems affecting the appropriateness of universalism which I propose in this article, for all intents and purposes, is also an attempt to think about human rights both globally and locally and, therefore, it is also an answer to the critiques of *both* realists and differentialists.

That said, I shall concentrate explicitly on issues of cross-cultural acceptance of human rights which consists in making a commitment to universalism compatible with the fact of cultural diversity (Teson 1985, Taylor 1996). Simply stated the problem consists in considering the practice of human rights capable of being endorsed by a set of different moral, metaphysical and cultural points of view. Notoriously, Jacques Maritain, the French Catholic philosopher member of the UNESCO Committee on Human Rights after the Second World War said – speaking of the theoretical bases of human rights – that 'we agree about the rights but on condition that no one asks us why'. By this he meant that human rights are 'practical conclusions which, although justified in different ways by different persons, are principles of action with a common ground of similarity for everyone' (Maritain 1949, pp. 9, 10). So, the idea that international human rights as a public doctrine are open to a variety of justifications – which I endorse – is not new and has some respectable pedigree.

The conundrum present in this view is clear: human rights are supposed to be 'universal' but it is not clear in what sense. *Prima facie* we can say that their universality implies that many values embodied in the human rights doctrine can be seen as important for all human beings, independently of their institutional and cultural ties. The philosophical puzzles come after the concern that there is no sufficient justification for this claim. In particular we can suppose that the normative practice of human rights is not neutral among the main metaphysical and moral conceptions across the various societies and cultures of the planet. If true, the proclamation and enforcement of human rights would be an act of disrespect and intolerance for all those cultures in which human rights norms are not easily accepted.

Pluralist integration from below and global overlapping consensus

There certainly may be – I maintained – different justifications for any one institutional practice, but they can be unified under a factual–normative legitimation. This process goes through a series of stages. In my interpretation, the first of these stages is of a political nature, while the second tries to deepen the theoretical nature of the process via the idea of a global overlapping consensus. Let me expand on this claim.

As argued elsewhere (Maffettone 2006), building on the recognition of the fact of cultural diversity at the global level, a promising approach is what I call 'pluralist integration from below'. On this view, human rights, just like any other fundamental matter as political democracy and the rule of law, may not be asserted by only one part of the world system and then exported abroad. Quite the contrary. Since their success depends on the possibility of their becoming the heritage of individual national cultures, reasons in their support should be found within local cultural backgrounds. In other words, a plurality of reasons in support of human rights, and other fundamental political matters, should be integrated as they emerge from different cultural backgrounds.

Now, this seems to be a politically reasonable proposal. If it is meaningless to impose supposedly Western certainties on members of cultures that do not perceive them as such, it does not make much sense, on the other hand, to 'sanctify' local cultures, abstaining from a critical evaluation of their contents. In any event, the necessity to balance these two needs and the political reasonableness of the approach I endorse say nothing on its philosophical cogency. It is one of my main aims in this article to outline a philosophical argument consistent with the *prima facie* reasonable political approach of a pluralist integration from below.

The pluralist integration model I endorse suggests a specific way to realize an overlapping consensus on human rights (Cohen 2004). As is well-known, reaching an overlapping consensus presupposes the existence of only one and the same institutional structure, support from which may be drawn from different moral, religious and metaphysical perspectives (Rawls 1993, lecture IV). Within this institutional structure, different comprehensive doctrines can coexist in a regime of reasonable pluralism and mutual tolerance. Such an account of the overlapping consensus is clearly historically contextualized within the nation-state. Within the boundaries of the nation-state, structured as a well-ordered society (Rawls 1993, pp. 35–40), it is plausible to think that the majority of conflicts between different doctrines are partial (or 'reasonable', to use Rawls's standard term). In other words, it is plausible to presume that everybody can accept the institutional framework within which these conflicts take place, without renouncing his or her profoundly held comprehensive view. However, the same strategy does not seem *prima facie* applicable to the international arena, where there is no such a thing as a common institutional framework to uphold.

This mismatch between the standard notion of overlapping consensus – connected with the idea of nation-state – and what we can call global overlapping consensus is evident if we reflect upon the origin and the structure of the standard notion. Rawls's overlapping consensus is realized when citizens adhering to different comprehensive doctrines accept the same liberal political outlook in a well-ordered society. Such a convergence is not imposed on citizens from above, but takes place for each citizen 'from within their own comprehensive view', building on 'the religious, philosophical and moral grounds it provides' (Rawls 1993, p. 147). Each citizen, regardless of whether his or her basic comprehensive doctrine is Muslim or Catholic, secular or Buddhist, utilitarian or Kantian, sceptical or pluralist, should reach an agreement on the principles of liberal and egalitarian political justice, finding some of the reasons to do so within his or her own comprehensive doctrine. The resulting consensus, according to Rawls, is not a superficial or prudential agreement, but is rather of a moral nature. We are not faced with compromise, with what Rawls calls a mere 'modus vivendi'.

The basic intention consists in breaking down the morality of individuals into two parts. On the one hand, there is the morality of persons viewed as a whole, which rests upon deep ethical or religious foundations; on the other hand, there is a more limited institutional morality, which concerns citizens rather than individuals and is not rooted in the ethical or religious depths of each person, but rather in the loyalty of everybody to the political and constitutional system in which they live their public lives. The political conception of justice based on the institutional morality makes it possible to govern the pluralism of the conceptions of the good. This occurs precisely through the formation of an *overlapping consensus* among citizens, who – although they remain rooted in their ultimate convictions and, indeed, nurture themselves with them – are nevertheless capable of placing them aside in the public sphere (better, in certain aspects of the public sphere) and accepting a common and predominant institutional morality.

So the core idea coincides here with the creation of this institutional morality. It reasserts Rawls's commitment to the priority of the right over the good. In a well-ordered society pluralism reigns supreme. Different aesthetic, ethical and religious views meet and confront each other. But pluralism cannot concern the entire institutional order and the fundamental structures of politics. Here, on the contrary, we all need a certain degree of unity. This unity, however, cannot be founded on a single ethical and political theory. In this case, therefore, we need a consensus that is less deep but broader, whose primary object is precisely a political conception of justice capable of allowing a basic structure that can ensure pluralism to a certain extent.

Many scholars have been perplexed with respect to the solution of an overlapping consensus as proposed by Rawls. The reason for such a distrust in Rawls's solution often lies in the double standard with which Rawls seems to view disagreements concerning the conception of the good and disagreements concerning the conception of justice. For some critics, Rawls seems to immunise unduly the notion of justice from conflict. The praise of pluralism seems limited to the disagreements about the good. But then the 'shared convictions', the 'fundamental ideas', the 'political conception' and, even more so, the 'overlapping consensus', seem to confirm the impression that, faced with deep disagreements on the good, there is a certain unity of view on at least several general characteristics of justice.

Hence, the reaction of the critics: is it possible to conceive a world, such as the one we live in, without thinking of it in the light of robust conflicts of a political and moral nature on justice? The negative answer to this type of question is the reason why the promoters of the typical objections to Rawls propound the two principal critical options: either the immunisation of politics occurs through a de facto compromise, a modus vivendi, or Rawls formulates another version of a liberal 'comprehensive doctrine'.

I believe that to respond to these objections it will be necessary to think that one can simultaneously maintain two interpretations of liberalism. In the first, liberalism is viewed as a comprehensive doctrine, and we could positively identify it with (an interpretation of) Rawls's theory of justice as fairness, but also with a Kantian conception based on autonomy, or yet something else again. This interpretation of liberalism, however, concerns only the level of 'justification', which is grounded in a comprehensive doctrine. This level is exposed to the attacks from the 'existence of pluralism' positions. If we were to move only at this level, it would be impossible to find convergence upon justice. But we can nonetheless resort to a second meaning of liberalism, based on the principle of 'legitimation'. In short, this second idea of liberalism suggests that there are liberal democratic institutions and practices that no 'reasonable' person would want to do without. These are few and fundamental and concern the essential elements of a liberal constitution and matters of basic justice. My argument is that the overlapping consensus can exist only insofar as it unites these two views of liberalism, the one based on justification and the other based on legitimation.

Reference to legitimation is important as it takes into account – as cherished by Habermas and Rawls – elements of historical experience capable, so to speak, of qualifying consensus with the support of external factors someway independent of the favoured theoretical approach. Accordingly, the way out from the above dilemma can only be inspired by actual experience, which, in the public domain, is constituted by the way in which the basic structure functions in the ambit of a liberal–democratic system

The basic structure argument

Overlapping consensus – as presented in the previous section – concerns justificatory pluralism but only within the nation-state. The problem I address in this article concerns expanding this model to the global setting. Here one faces a well-known difficulty. The alleged impossibility of a global overlapping consensus derives from the problems encountered by the straightforward application of Rawls's basic structure argument (BSA) to global justice.[5] For Rawls the 'basic structure' includes the group of the major institutions of a society and is the main subject of a theory of justice. In Rawls's words, 'the primary subject of justice is the basic structure of society, or more exactly, the way in which the major social institutions distribute fundamental rights and duties and determine the division of advantages from social cooperation' (Rawls 1971, p. 7). The BSA can be summarized as follows:

(i) justice requires the existence of the basic structure as its precondition;
(ii) the basic structure applies only to national societies; *therefore*
(iii) there is no justice beyond national societies.

This *prima facie* argument requires further investigation. The BSA says that obligations of justice are not conceivable outside the domain of the nation-state because the nation-state does correspond to our intuitive conception of a basic structure. If we reflect on this intuitive conception however we see that it is not necessarily true. The problem of global justice – once exposed to a more serious reflection – appears to be a problem of 'scope': justice does not apply outside a determined institutional context and we must decide how large has to be the scope of it. One can accept that this scope does correspond to the site determined by the notion of basic structure, but it is not at all said that the scope of the basic structure necessarily corresponds to the nation-state. There are plenty of human relationships that exceed the dimensions of a nation-state and this network of relationships can be the background for imagining an alternative view of the basic structure whose scope is larger than the nation-state. And if we are not satisfied by solving the question of the scope of our obligations of justice by the identification of the basic structure with the nation-state, then we must look for a ground for an alternative solution to this conundrum (among others, see Nagel 2005, Cohen and Sabel 2006, Blake 2001, Sangiovanni 2007, Risse 2006, Abizadeh 2007, and Julius 2003).

For the BSA, obligations of justice are grounded in some public system of imposition of morally relevant norms. On this presupposition, the discussion on the ground on which one is supposed to base obligations of global justice can be put in terms of 'relationalism' starting from a distinction between relational and non-relational approaches.[6] Relational approaches maintain that obligations of justice are triggered by relevant social relationships. Non-relational approaches maintain that obligations of justice apply to human beings as such, independently from social relationships.

For non-relational approaches, there is no special problem in making obligations of justice correspond to some idea of global justice. For relational approaches, however, the same task becomes more complicated. Scholars in favour of relational approaches must specify what kind of relevant social relationships and institutional background is required to trigger proper obligations of justice. From this specification they will derive the nature, the scope and the ground of principles of justice. In this light we can reformulate the BSA.

There are two different possible readings of the BSA. On the first strict reading (BSA1), the existence itself of the basic structure includes significant normative elements. It is in some way moralized. The basic structure exists to favour social cooperation, but – on this understanding – social cooperation is meant to be 'fair' social cooperation. On this strict reading, the existential condition of the basic structure coincides with its own moralized version. The conclusion is that where there are not yet fair terms of cooperation – like in the global setting – justice does not apply. On the second, more 'tolerant' reading (BSA2), one can distinguish between the existence of the basic structure and the significance of some demands of justice independently from its full moral version. Demands of justice can exist even if there is no prior presence of 'fair' terms of cooperation. The mere fact that there is social cooperation – as is certainly the case in the global arena – might create sensible demands of justice. I find BSA2 more plausible: obligations of justice do respond to demands of justice.

On these grounds, I reject the BSA impossibility theorem concerning a global overlapping consensus on fundamental human rights. If we assume – as it seems customary to do – that human rights are not only a set of moral imperatives but also a set of legal requisites (for this double standard of human rights, see Nickel 1987, and Shue 1996), then we can maintain that this set of legal norms constitute a formidable shared background available to all cultures.[7] It is actually quite difficult even to think that one can replace the existing human rights with a different set of moral imperatives, capable (at least in principle) of defending and protecting human dignity but lacking such a historically successful *pedigree*. This conclusion has two major implications: first, it seems apparent that different moralities, religions and metaphysics can well ground the same set of human rights; second, it is equally evident that none of such different moralities, religions and metaphysics could play the same function that the existing set of human rights is currently playing. In other words, it seems more promising to strive for accommodating different religions, moralities and metaphysics within the existing set of human rights than *vice versa*. The integration of an already existing platform of human rights and several profound justifications for them must however be in my view pluralist and critical. This means that existing human rights – as we shall see below – cannot be taken for granted and their legitimating force must be discussed and evaluated by an open cross-cultural dialogue. This is the extent to which I think the idea of an overlapping consensus can be fruitfully applied to the foundation of human rights.

In keeping with Rawls's teaching, the fundamental philosophical idea that underlies this approach to the foundation of human rights concerns each person's double loyalty, at an ethical/metaphysical and at a political level. At an ethical and metaphysical level, each maintains his or her own traditional cultural and religious perspective but, at the same time, at a political level, s/he chooses a vision that is convergent with that of the other members of the international community, through the progressive affirmation of a sort of multicultural overlapping consensus. According to the overlapping consensus thesis applied to human rights, human rights are shared elements, of legal and political nature, consistent with various moral, religious and metaphysical foundations. Hence, my argument presupposes the existence of a critical potential inherent to all cultures that, eventually, will cause them to converge partially in the direction desired by the advocates of human rights.

My argument makes it possible to reconcile two contrasting views concerning the cross-cultural foundation of human rights. According to one view, cultural sensitivity to local traditions should override the universality of human rights; according to the other, it is the universality of human rights which is supposed to override local traditions. Combining the commitment to pluralist integration from below with the idea of an overlapping consensus via a 'tolerant' interpretation of the basic structure argument (which I called BSA2), my argument aims at reconciling these two contrasting views at a higher level.

The theoretical model

Applying the distinction between justification and legitimation to the human rights issue is crucial as a strategy for the reconciliation of its (more) philosophical aspects (justification) and its (more) empirical aspects (legitimation). However differently from the theoretical models presented by Rawls and Habermas, issues of justification and of legitimation are not clearly distinguished in the case at hand. To clarify, a further distinction must be drawn between two types of justification strategies – call them 'justification A' and 'justification B' – and two types of legitimation strategies – call them 'legitimation A' and 'legitimation B'. I propose to conceive of justification A as a typically philosophical strategy endowed with a distinctive moral nature. Justification A addresses the totality of human subjects in a universalistic fashion. Potentially, no human being is excluded from it. We shall say that *justification A is universal*. Justification B, on the other hand, belongs to the argumentative toolkit, as it were, of a strategy based on the idea of an overlapping consensus, as explained above. Justification B aims at rooting justification A in the basic metaphysical premises that characterize every culture. In this sense, justification B is culturally sensitive and it can draw both from religious and secular traditions. Thus interpreted, *justification B is special*.

Similarly, legitimation strategies may be accounted for in analogous dual terms. What I have called legitimation A refers to an empirical, extensive agreement on existing institutions and practices, as for example on a shared set of human rights as presented in the 1948 UN Declaration. As anticipated, the UN Declaration is taken to be the object of a widespread agreement involving almost all people on earth. As a consequence of its enjoying such a wide historically constructed legitimation, any alternative set of human rights cannot be plausibly thought to succeed in replacing the existing one in a reasonable time. On this ground, I shall say that *legitimation A is general* (as far as it depends on the generalized consent of people on earth). Legitimation B is path dependent. It clearly depends on the history of the consent on human rights in different cultures and traditions, typically on the way in which these cultures and traditions have been able to revise their own basic assumptions to converge on human rights, as internationally recognized and legally established. However, legitimation B has to do with the actual practices and institutions through which human rights are accepted and implemented within different cultural contexts. In this sense, *legitimation B is local.*

To recapitulate, we should operate the following distinctions:

- (I) Justification
  - (IA) universal justification
  - (IB) special justification
- (II) Legitimation
  - (IIA) general legitimation
  - (IIB) local legitimation

Justification and legitimation can thus be integrated, allowing a philosophically grounded reconciliation of the universalist and culturally specific concerns that have animated large part of the debate on this issue. As already suggested, my argument presupposes the existence of an underlying critical potential in every tradition and culture. The presence of this critical potential substantiates my favourite approach to the foundation of human rights, what I have called 'pluralist integration from below'.

Literally understood, pluralist integration from below implies that such fundamental political matters as human rights, political democracy and the rule of law may not be imposed from the outside but, on the contrary, must be grounded in and realized through resources available from within different cultures. This is essential to allow the legitimation processes at work in different cultures (legitimation B) to succeed in affirming similar human rights, the content of (but not the justifications for) which is inspired by the principles of liberalism. The last step to take is to look closer at how such a pluralist integration from below may operate and be realized from a cross-cultural perspective.

Back to the world

The political scheme I have illustrated building on the idea of a pluralist integration from below aims at reconciling the universal and the local aspects of the human rights discourse. It does so by recognizing the importance of cultural diversity while mitigating such a recognition through the assumption of a partial convergence on certain well known forms of protection of the human being. It is interesting to note that, as we move from the purely cultural level to the level of the institutionalization of fundamental human rights, my assumption is strongly confirmed. The historical realization of human rights has been undoubtedly conditioned by the legal and institutional practices to which we are familiar across the globe. On the other hand, human rights represent ethical limits to what local practices and institutions may do. From this point of view, the goal of setting these limits may be attained by recourse to a number of different institutional tools, depending on the political, legal and social contexts under consideration. Such a variety of institutionalization tools are part and parcel of the idea of there being an overlapping consensus on human rights in different traditions.

The force of my proposal may also be appreciated by adopting a classical hermeneutical methodology. From this perspective, human rights need to be adjusted to actual circumstances, starting from the procedures and the rules of the system where they are to be applied. In this way, application processes require as a matter of necessity a hermeneutically relevant translation of normative meanings. Such a translation accounts for the *Wirkungeschichtlichkeit* – the historical effectiveness – of reference to different contexts with respect to the assumed universality of human rights.

Until now, my discussion of human rights and cultural diversity has been very abstract. However, many of the claims requiring a cross-cultural perspective are empirical claims changing from place to place and through time. My argument has shown that Western liberalism is not the only plausible foundation for human rights because – through reference to an overlapping consensus of different culturally embedded justifications – we can rely on other philosophical, religious and cultural traditions. This said, by moving from theory to practice, a problem may arise: there are surely cases in which what human rights substantially dictate comes to conflict with the philosophical–religious practices and convictions of other cultures. This has been frequently considered the case with reference to Islam and the so-called Asian values. Insofar as such traditions (allegedly) at odds with the demands of human rights are widespread in certain areas and provide overriding reasons for action for many persons, it is not clear how and why human rights should prevail over them in case of conflict. It is also important to note that this kind of potential conflict is not new. In the 1940s, the UNESCO Committee, while the Declaration was being drafted, had already posed this problem. As mentioned above, on that occasion, Maritain suggested resolving this problem by considering that a general consensus on what human rights are recognized in practice can coexist with disagreement on the reasons why any given human right is considered as such from a foundational point of view. In the same spirit, and vis-à-vis the renewed urgency the problem has recently acquired, I have tried to strike a balance between human rights' claims to universality and attention to cultural pluralism and contextualism.

How does this complex methodological approach relate to concrete cross-cultural questions? I would like to offer an example in connection with the supposed incompatibility between human rights and the so-called Asian values. After the climax of 1993, the debate revolving around Asian values became less lively. Reference to such values has become less and less common during a transformation process which goes hand in hand with the 'democratic revival' of many Asian countries. It must be also noted that, in recent years, the attempt by many Asian countries to create a sort of regional Asian politics changed in a substantial way. Year after year, requisites such as respect for human rights and democracy became, so to say, less global and more local. Interestingly, the more Western nations relaxed their pressure to encourage Asian countries to respect human rights and implement democracy, the more Asian nations started doing so by themselves. The reasons behind such a trend among Asian nations oscillate between the will to respect the needs of a more mature civil society and the necessity to control social conflicts. Whatever reason behind this phenomenon, a new interest in human rights and in defending democracy becomes evident in the regional politics of many Asian nations. In 2005, the Kuala Lumpur Declaration on the establishment of an Association of Southeast Asian Nations (ASEAN) Charter embodied for the first time a commitment to promoting democracy, human rights and good governance. At the same time, as the military regime of Myanmar decided to relinquish its turn as ASEAN's chairmanship in 2006, there were pressures to expel Myanmar from ASEAN if the military regime was not able to improve its human rights record. All this seems to suggest that the structural conflict between Asian identity and human rights, such as that prospected by the original Asian values debate, has been in some way overcome and transformed.

This new trend in Asian regionalism seems to reveal two major failures. On the one hand, what failed was the attempt of Western countries to impose human rights from above and outside local cultures. This attempt was in some way both naive and imperialistic. It overlooked the national interests of the Asian countries and their reasonable postcolonial (re)sentment. Both their interests and resentment were of course corroborated by a new sense of force due to the impressive economic progress in South East Asia in the last decades. This successful resistance to the Western imposition of the human rights platform has been celebrated in the Asian values debate. On the other hand, as I just said, the same Asian values debate did not succeed in driving a wedge between the culture of human rights and Asian identity. On the contrary, the more Asian nations tried to reconstruct their collective identity, the more the need to respect human rights and protect democracy appeared as a necessary condition for such a collective enterprise (Bauer and Bell 1999).

The reconstruction of the history of Asian politics in recent years seems to provide empirical support to my favoured approach to the foundation of human rights: pluralist integration from below, modelled according to the idea of an overlapping consensus articulated through the dialectics between justification and legitimation. The Western attempt to impose human rights from above and outside may be seen as an attempt to realize what I called justification A (universal justification) without coupling it with a parallel process rooted in legitimation B (local legitimation). In other words, without a serious internal revision of local practices, in which legitimation B consists, the universal value of human rights (justification A) could not be realized.

The failure of the 'Asian values strategy', based on the separation between the human rights perspective and Asian identity, exemplifies another important part of my model. Here, it is the attempt to validate justification B (special justification) for example by invoking the Confucian philosophy as done by former Prime Minister of Singapore Lee to show that with no reference to legitimation A, namely the fact that the UN Declaration has had a large impact on the world culture, justification B cannot work properly. The regionalization strategy of the last years brought about new forms of cross-cultural dialogue due to the global roots of the contemporary Asian civil society. This dialogical interaction is the main source of integration of strategies of justification A and legitimation B (grounding universalism in local cultural practices), and of legitimation A and justification B (by connecting local justifications to shared global institutionalized principles).

In light of the above, it is necessary to recognize the complex and mutable character of the human rights discourse. The formulation of fundamental human rights is inescapably affected, in a manner that defies any a priori determination, by a web of legitimations and justifications in specific historical and normative contexts mediated by cross-cultural dialogue. Such an argument is developed in response to two imperatives: one related to substance and one to method. From the substantive point of view, the idea is that the interpretation and foundation of human rights, as they are usually conceived in the international context, should be mediated by consideration of a complex network of cultures and historical situations. Otherwise, human rights are at risk of never taking root, particularly within societies where many social classes have experienced a hastily forced Westernization. At the same time, human rights constitute a limit to cultural self-leniency, that is to say, they put the brakes on the temptation to believe that all that comes from one's own tradition is as such automatically permitted.

Acknowledgements

This paper was originally given at the 'Respect, Global Justice and Human Rights' conference held at the University of Pavia in 2009. I am particularly grateful to Emanuela Ceva and Ian Carter for the opportunity to present it in this optimal setting and for numerous comments. For their comments during the conference, I also thank Simon Caney, Darrell Moellendorf and Zaid Eyadat. This paper took advantage of the discussion with Gianfranco Pellegrino, Domenico Melidoro and Valentina Gentile in my department at LUISS, University in Rome. A special thank you to the anonymous referee for many helpful comments.

Notes

1. An interesting view from the perspective of the excluded is given by Tibebu (2011). The Eurocentrism of Hegel's thesis is convincingly revealed by Chakrabatry (2011).
2. Notable exceptions are Simmons (2001), but – as will become apparent – my proposal is significantly different from his; and Buchanan (2002), who speaks of legitimacy from a normative point of view but in terms of the monopoly of political power.
3. The parallel way in which Habermas and Rawls – each in his own way – combine justification and legitimation can be taken as a consequence of a larger project of institutionalization of reason that they both independently share. Both Habermas and Rawls derive such a project from the 'proceduralization' of the Kantian categorical imperative as is explicitly recognized by Rawls (1971, section 40).
4. Beitz says that this practice is 'emergent' – and for this very reason not mature – precisely because human rights are not always respected even if some level of compliance is necessary for the existence of the practice itself.
5. My discussion of the BSA is inspired by Abizadeh (2007) (also Nagel 2005, Cohen and Sabel 2006, Blake 2001, Risse 2006, Julius 2003).
6. I take this distinction from Sangiovanni (2007). Instead of 'relationalism' one can opt also for 'associativism', as in Moellendorf (2002).
7. I do not discuss here the issue concerning the possibility of having legal norms that are not easily enforceable like human rights because it seems both unnecessary from the point of view of this paper and very empirically complex. I simply maintain that the conception of human rights as a practice permits them to be considered among the customary sources of international law.

References

Abizadeh, A., 2007. Cooperation, pervasive impact, and coercion: on the scope (not site) of distributive justice. *Philosophy and Public Affairs*, 35, 318–358.

Bauer, J. R. and Bell, D. A., eds., 1999. *The East Asian challenge for human rights*. Cambridge: Cambridge University Press.

Beitz, C., 2009. *The idea of human rights*. Oxford: Oxford University Press.

Blake, M., 2001. Distributive justice, state coercion and autonomy. *Philosophy and Public Affairs*, 30, 257–296.
Buchanan, A., 2002. Political legitimacy and democracy. *Ethics*, 112, 689–719.
Chakrabatry, D., 2011. *Provincializing Europe: postcolonial thought and historical difference*. Princeton, NJ: Princeton University Press.
Cohen, J., 2004. Minimalism about human rights: the most we can hope for? *Journal of Political Philosophy*, 12 (2), 190–213.
Cohen, J. and Sabel, C., 2006. Extra rempublicam nulla justitia. *Philosophy and Public Affairs*, 34, 147–175.
Cornell, D., Rosenfeld, M., and Carlson, D. G., eds, 1992. *Deconstruction and the possibility of justice*. New York, NY: Routledge.
Cranston, M., 1973. *What are human rights?* Revd edn. New York, NY: New York University Press.
Glendon, M. A., 2001. *A world made new: Eleanor Roosevelt and the Universal Declaration of Human Rights*. New York, NY: Random House.
Habermas, J., 1996. *Between facts and norms, Contributions to a discourse theory of law and democracy*. Cambridge, MA: MIT Press.
Julius, A. J., 2003. Basic structure and the value of equality. *Philosophy and Public Affairs*, 31, 31–55.
Maffettone, S., 2006. *La pensabilita del mondo*. Milan: Il Saggiatore.
Maffettone, S., 2010. *Rawls: an introduction*. Cambridge: Polity.
Maffettone, S., 2011. How to avoid the liaison dangereuse between post-colonialism and post-modernism. *Philosophy and Social Criticism*, 37 (4), 493–504.
Maritain, J., 1949. Introduction. *In*: *UNESCO, Human rights: comments and interpretations*. London: Allan Wingate.
Moellendorf, D., 2002. *Cosmopolitan justice*. Boulder, CO: Westview.
Nagel, T., 2005. The problem of global justice. *Philosophy and Public Affairs*, 33, 113–147.
Nickel, J. M., 1987. *Making sense of human rights*. Berkeley, CA: University of California Press.
Rawls, J., 1971. *A theory of justice*. Oxford: Oxford University Press.
Rawls, J., 1993. *Political liberalism*. New York, NY: Columbia University Press.
Rawls, J., 1999. *Collected papers*. Cambridge, MA: Harvard University Press.
Risse, M., 2006. What to say about the state. *Social Theory and Practice*, 32, 671–698.
Sangiovanni, A., 2007. Global justice, reciprocity and the state. *Philosophy and Public Affairs*, 35, 2–39.
Sen, A., 2009. *The idea of justice*. Cambridge, MA: Belknap.
Shue, H., 1996. *Basic rights*. Princeton, NJ: Princeton University Press.
Simmons, A. J., 2001. *Justification and legitimacy, Essays on rights and obligations*. Cambridge: Cambridge University Press.
Taylor, C., 1996. A world consensus on human rights. *Dissent*, Summer, 15–21.
Teson, F. R., 1985. International human rights and cultural relativism. *Virginia Journal of International Law*, 25 (4), 869–898.
Tibebu, T., 2011. *Hegel and the Third World*. New York, NY: Syracuse University Press.

Index

Page numbers in **Bold** represent figures.